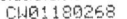

The Reality of Real Estate Investing

By

Allen Watkins

© 2001 by Allen Watkins. All rights reserved.

No part of this book may be reproduced, stored in a retrieval system, or transmitted by any means, electronic, mechanical, photocopying, recording, or otherwise, without written permission from the author.

ISBN: 0-75964-093-9

This book is printed on acid free paper.

1stBooks – rev. 05/11/01

Real Estate Investing has a long tradition of helping people gain wealth & financial freedom.

A trip of a 1000 miles begins with a single step.

Your journey to financial independence begins now!

This publication is designed to provide accurate and authoritative information, not legal advice. Events and laws may change after publication. The author and publisher specifically disclaim any liability, loss, risk, personal or otherwise, which is incurred as a consequence, directly or indirectly, of the use and application of any of the contents of this work. Before acting on any suggestion presented in this book, legal or other professional assistance may be advisable.

Acknowledgements

First and foremost, I give thanks to our Heavenly Father and our Savior Jesus Christ who gives us all we have and makes it possible for us to achieve success.

I dedicate this book to my wife Debra, my sons Dexter, Dustin, and Christopher. They fulfil my life and give meaning to it.

I give thanks to my wife for her enduring support in my endeavors to succeed.

Thanks to Gary Furstenfeld, who became my mentor when I was starting out by providing me guidance and direction..

Thanks to Mike Boren who was one of my first financial partners. For his confidence, support and trust over the years.

Thanks to my brokerage business partner Bruce Sonnenberg for his talents in helping make that business a success. And allowing me the time to complete this valuable work.

Thanks to Ethel Guernsey for her enduring labor in proof reading and correcting my grammar.

Thanks to Leopoldo Herman and Mark Kime for their assistance in helping me complete this work.

Thanks to my many friends and associates for their input in the preparation of this work.

Thanks to each of you who do not merely read the words enclosed herein, but actually put them into practice. It is you who actually makes this effort a success!

Preface

When I first started in the real estate business, I had the guidance and direction of a mentor. However, he did not hold my hand. I had to learn much through trial and error. I read books and attended real estate seminars. Although, I picked up some useful information, much of it I thought was puff and fluff. It seemed to be more hype and not enough meat and potatoes.

One day when I had taken some time off work and was relaxing at my brother Hugh's home in Tennessee, it hit me strong and hard. I now had been in the business about ten years and, having achieved a degree of success, was pondering my experiences. That is when the spark of inspiration ignited in me to write a book. I wanted to provide detailed information in helping others understand and achieve what I had done. I know there are many people out there who show an interest and desire to invest in real estate because I have met them at seminars and through my business. However, 95% of them never do anything with their desire. Perhaps it is because of the lack of knowledge being made easily available.

I knew I could make that information available.

This is not just surface information or bits and pieces of information, but it is detailed indepth information, everything someone would need to know to make it happen. It is all the information I wished was available to me when I was starting out.

It is truly magnificent setting forth a strategy to accomplish one's desires and then to achieve them. It is good to experience the degrees of success along the way. Memorable events are the first face to face appointment, the first offer, negotiating, the first acceptance of an offer, acquiring the money necessary, the first closing or successful bid, competing right up with there with the already successful, and rubbing shoulders with them.

A satisfaction of accomplishment is felt in taking a beat-up house and turning it into a nice home for a family to live in and enjoy. Also, in paying your financial partner back as agreed or sooner, getting your first check of profit, helping a fellow human being turn his negative circumstances into a positive one, rescuing an abandoned pet, owning your first apartment building and your first commercial building, etc.

All these give you more than monetary gain; you achieve a sense of accomplishment that is indescribable and truly worthwhile. However, that is not all; then it is our nature to always want to go the next step, that next level of effort, accomplishment, and success. For me that is helping others to achieve success as I have. Thus, the purpose of my writing this book. Good Luck!

The only way to make our future better than our present,

is to do things differently in our present,
than we did in our past.

Table of Contents

CHAPTER ONE 1

MOTIVATED SELLERS

- Why Real Estate? 1
- Sources 2
- Foreclosures 3
- The Myth About Foreclosures 4
- Consider the Alternative 4
- Communicating with the Occupant 5
- Reasons for Foreclosure 6

CHAPTER TWO 9

THE FORECLOSURE PROCESS

- Trustee's Deed 10
- Note and Mortgage 11
- Security Deed 11
- Lien versus Title 11
- Power of Sale 11
- Various Methods of Foreclosure Nationwide 12
- Mortgage versus Trust Deed Foreclosure 12
- The Judicial Process 13

　　　* The First Stage / Filing of the Lis Pendens

- The Second Stage 14

　　　* Order of Judgment and Order for Sale
　　　* Redemption Period

- The Third Stage 14

　　　* The Auction
　　　　- Sheriff's Sale
　　　　- Commissioners Sale
　　　　- Private Entities

ix

- The Fourth Stage 17
- The Trustee Sale Process 18
- The Home Equity Sales Law 20
- How to Read Default Notices 21

CHAPTER THREE 24

RESEARCH

- Lead Gathering 24

    * Legal Notices 24
    * County Court House 24
        - The Complaint of Foreclosure
        - The Summons

    * Private Entities 26
    * Banks or Lending Institutions 26
    * HUD And VA 27
    * Realtors 27

- Pinpoint the Numbers 28

    * Acquisition Cost
    * Holding Cost
    * Remodeling Cost and Maintenance
    * Selling Cost
    * Closing Cost

- Preparing To Bid 29
- Properties Not Bid On 30

CHAPTER FOUR 31

APPROACHING THE OWNER

- Contacting the Owner 31

    * Appearance

- The Introduction 32

x

- ♦ When Vacant 32

    * Death
    * Jail
    * Fear
    * Transfer
    * Bad Memories

- ♦ Locating the Owner 33

    * Writing Letters
    * Questions to Ask

CHAPTER FIVE 38

MAKING DEALS / MONEY WITH THE OWNER

- ♦ Profit Centers 38

    * Management Technique
    * Purchase
    * Selling
    * Sale / Lease Back with Option
    * Referral

CHAPTER SIX 46

APPROACHING THE LENDER

- ♦ Contact Sources 47
    * Yellow Pages
    * Home Owners / Foreclosure Legal Notice
    * Calling the Attorney
    * Lender Directories
    * Walk Right into a Bank

CHAPTER SEVEN 51

MAKING DEALS / MONEY WITH LENDERS

- ♦ Purchasing / Discounting the Mortgage 51

- Buying Before the Auction 52
- Buying at the Auction 53
- Buying after the Auction 53
- Working with Realtors 54

CHAPTER EIGHT 56

CREATIVE FINANCING

- A Little Personal History 56
- No Money Down 57
- Creativity is the Key 58

   * Secure Card
   * Finance Companies
   * Banks

- Sources for Active Investors 61

   * Partners
   * Family and Friends
   * Paper Money

- First Right of Refusal 64
- Financial Resume Profile 64
- Mortgage Hunting Tips 65

   * Cash Back
   * Time Ownership Limitation
   * Portfolio Lender
   * Loan to Value Ratio
   * Terms
   * Amortization
   * Walk Away Power

CHAPTER NINE 68

SUCCESSFUL TENANT MANAGEMENT

- Tenant / Landlord Relations 69
- Determining Rent Amount 69

- ♦ Finding a Tenant 69
- ♦ Screening Tenants 70

  * Section 8 Tenants
  * Disabled Tenants
  * Questions To Ask
  * Playing Detective

- ♦ In-Home Inspection 74
- ♦ Security Deposit 75
- ♦ The Rental Agreement 76
- ♦ Move-in Inspection 76
- ♦ Resident Policy & Regulations 76
- ♦ When Tenants Go Bad 79
- ♦ Insurance 80
- ♦ Property Taxes 81

  * Market Value
  * Assessed Value
  * Equalization Factor
  * Tax Rate
  * Are you Over-Assessed?
  * Valuation and Tax Rate Protest

- ♦ Bookkeeping 86
- ♦ Smoke Detector Agreement 88
- ♦ Rent Credit Program 89

CHAPTER TEN 90

CONTRACTORS

- ♦ Types of contractors 90

  * Rip-off Artist
  * Jack-of-all-Trades
  * General and Sub-Contractors
  * The Handyman

- ♦ Locating Contractors 91

- Best Sources to Pursue 92
- Questions to Ask a Contractor 92
- Inspecting the Contractor's Work 94
- Some things to look for: 94
- The Contractor Agreement 95

  * Itemized Bid
  * Paying the Contractor
  * Labor Money
  * Useful Clauses

- Obtain Knowledge 99
- Do Not Relinquish Control 99

CHAPTER ELEVEN 101

REMODELING AND MAINTENANCE

- Lower Priced Homes 102
- Patching vs Replacing 102
- Middle Priced Homes 104
- Upper Priced Homes 104
- General Tips 105
- Maintenance 107
- Routine Maintenance 107

CHAPTER TWELVE 109

CONTRACTS AND CLAUSES

- Attorney's Right to Review 109
- Minimum Essential Terms 111

  * Home Inspection Clause
  * Other Clauses
  * Earnest Money Clause

- License Tip 114
- Tax Tip 114

CHAPTER THIRTEEN 115

MARKETING STRATEGIES

- Preparing to Sell 115
- Pricing Your Home 117
- Comparable Market Analysis (C.M.A.) 118
- Marketing Activities 120

    * For Sale Sign
    * Safety Precautions
    * Advertising
    * Writing Advertising
    * Open Houses
    * Tips for planning an Open House
    * Neighborhood Canvassing
    * Bulletin Boards
    * Corporate Relocation Departments
    * Local Churches

- Qualifying Buyers 126

    * Show Your Home to Only Qualified Buyers
    * Questions to Ask
    * When a Buyer has a Home to Sell

- Your Financing Specialist 128
- To Hire an Attorney 129

CHAPTER FOURTEEN 131

NEGOTIATION

- Negotiating Tips 131

    * Building Rapport

- The First Offer 132
- When to Stop Talking 132
- Higher Authority / Good Guy - Bad Guy 133

* The Initial Walk Through
* Emotional Outbursts
* The Stall
*The Better Offer
* Split the Difference
* The Art of Flinching
*Divorcing Owners
* The Loan Extension
* The Right to Resell the Deal
* The First Right of Refusal
* Business not Emotional Decisions

CHAPTER FIFTEEN **139**

GET MOTIVATED

- Goals 139
- Exert Yourself Mentally 141

    * Your Mind's Eye
    * Auto Suggestion

- The Challenge 144

    * Discouragement
    * Procrastination

- Motivation 147

    * Attitude
    * Don't Quit
    * You
    * If You Think You Can't or Think You Can You Are Right
    * The Key To Success

CHAPTER SIXTEEN **154**

CASES IN POINT

1. Harlem 154
2. Hoyne 158

xvi

3. Forestville 159
4. Burbank 160
5. Barry 161
6. Hickory Hills 163
7. Streamwood 166
8. Rockwell 167
9. Foster Avenue 168
10. West Chicago 169
11. Summit 170
12. Evergreen Park 171
13. 76 Unit 172
14. Natchez 173
15. Dickens 173
16. 96th Place 173
17. Harvey 174
18. DesPlaines 175
19. Mohawk 175
20. Wentworth 176
21. Avers 177
22. Midlothian 178
23. Markham 178
24. Sauk Village 179
25. Crete 179

Glossary Of Real Estate Terms 181

Epilogue 185

The Virtual Reality of Real Estate Investing 189

About the Author 191

xvii

CHAPTER 1

Motivated Sellers

Why Real Estate?

There are many different sources to consider for investing money. The market provides stocks, bonds, commodities, precious gems, CD's, annuities, mutual funds, and business investment opportunities, etc. I personally choose Real Estate because it provides me with the greatest amount of flexibility and the opportunity for creativity.

In Real Estate I can make money while using my own money or by using other people's money. I also have the power! By that I mean I control the situation. What is happening in the economy has very little effect on my ability to make money. Most other investments involve basically turning your money over to someone else and then keeping your fingers crossed they make a decent return for you and do not lose your money. You see, people are always going to need a place to live. As long as you buy right, you have good security for your investment. You have the power! You decide how you want to remodel, whether you want to refinance and rent, or sell. Personally, I like being in control.

When people think of investing in Real Estate, most naturally they think of making money! People have different strategies on what they believe to be the best method for making money with Real Estate. There are those individuals who look at Real Estate investing as a source for a tax shelter or rate of return over time. There are also those who say the key to investing in real estate is "location, location, location." Buy in the right location and the value will increase year after year, or in real estate terms, appreciate in value.

That is fine for the investor who does not mind tying his money up and just earning a rate of return over time. I say the key to investing in real estate is by forcing appreciation.

- ♦ This is accomplished first and foremost by buying below market.
- ♦ Next you refinance to recoup your investment plus a profit that is tax free because it is borrowed money. You structure the deal so that the rental income covers the monthly mortgage payment, taxes, and insurance, while still leaving a positive cash flow.

- Or you put the property right back on the market and sell at or slightly below retail.
   See Case in Point # 16.

Now that is hundreds and sometimes thousands of percent rate of return. Take that same money and go do it again! I have done it over and over, and so can you.

My focus will be on buying at wholesale for immediate equity (profit) and selling at retail or holding, refinancing to pull your cash out along with a tax-free profit, and renting for cash flow, and if appreciation occurs then it is extra profit.

When I started in 1983, I had nothing. Therefore, for all of you who have nothing and do not have much in the way of cash flow out there, realize that all you really need is a positive attitude and the desire to put forth the effort to make it happen. Nothing just happens. You make it happen! Regardless of your life's circumstances, who you are, or where you are from, if you desire financial freedom, it can be yours!

Sources

In order to buy Real Estate below market value, you must locate a "Motivated Seller."

Some possible sources are:

- Drive around neighborhoods looking for property in need of repairs, with unkept yards, peeling paint, etc.
- Call listings in newspaper ads.

The first question to ask is, *"What is your reason for selling?"* Do not ask the address, price, or financing terms — only the motivation for selling. If the reason for selling is not one of motivation, say, *"My purpose for calling is from the point of view of an investor. I am looking for a seller who may be willing to sell for a lower price for cash and a quick closing, or perhaps close to the asking price with creative terms."* Speak slowly and clearly. Then be quiet. The silence may get uncomfortable, but wait for the seller's response. This response will help you determine if you should invest more time with this particular seller. If the seller asks specifically what you have in mind, you respond, *"Well, Mr. Seller, every situation is different. First, I would need to see your home."*

Most of the time the owners will disguise their reason for selling so as not to reveal their urgency. Of course, they are trying to prevent below market offers. It is not often you will call a seller who will admit he is really motivated and willing to sell below market. For this reason I do not go into more detail about dealing with these types of sellers. I encourage you to focus on sellers or potential sellers who we already know have motivation and need our help.

- Call on lenders. These are banks, mortgage companies, and finance companies. I will explain more about this in Chapter Six.
- The Multiple Listing Service (MLS). This, of course, is the Realtors' source of Real Estate for sale. Realtors are not usually too excited about presenting low ball or creative offers. When one is listed below market, it typically goes fast. Not many Realtors are involved in personal investing, but the ones who are usually are on the top of what comes their way. They, too, have limitations.

Opportunities are always there for those who are willing to search. No one person or one hundred persons can do it all. As my mentor said to me when I asked, *"Isn't there just too much competition for me to be able to get a piece of the action?"* he answered, *"Allen, there is always room for one more who is willing to put forth the effort to chase the deals."* With his guidance I proved him right! Now with my guidance so will you!

The properties that are in need of cosmetic work (general cleaning, painting, new carpet, minor repairs, landscaping, etc.) or rehabs (new cabinets, electric wiring, plumbing, heating, drywall, roofing, etc.) usually provide more opportunity to negotiate the price down or get creative terms. These are typically classified as fixer uppers, handyman specials, or rehabs.

The reality attitude for me about investing in Real Estate, is simply to buy as far below its actual value as possible, whether it needs work or is in move in condition. Although this is possible in the areas of endeavor discussed above, it is only logical to want to increase your percent of success by focusing where your best chance of success exists. After all, time is money. For most of us our time is limited, and our goal is to achieve maximum results for the time invested. This brings me to the subject of Foreclosures.

Foreclosures

This is where I have focused my attention because I already know there is motivation, urgency, and the greatest chance to buy real estate wholesale. There are different areas of foreclosure in which to profit. These are discussed in later chapters.

Allen Watkins

The Myth About Foreclosures

It seems that foreclosures have always been and always will be around. It is a part of human nature. As long as there are people experiencing up's and downs in their lives, there will be people not paying their mortgage and facing foreclosure.
What exactly is a foreclosure?

It is the legal means by which a lender using Real Estate as collateral may, upon delinquency or non-payment take away or have ownership of the Real Estate transferred to himself and away from the borrower.

This, of course, then gives the lender the right to sell the Real Estate and keep the proceeds - all the proceeds, even when there is substantial value above and beyond the debt. The profit gained is not always just monetary. Any personal property left behind with the Real Estate goes to the new owner as well. See Case in Point # 1, Harlem Ave.
There is an undeniable negative connotation in the minds of some individuals when you mention "Investing in Foreclosures." They picture you throwing a nice family of a husband, wife, and children out into the streets during the dead of winter. That scenario could not be further from the truth. I have had ownership of up to thirty two properties at one time and transactions on thousands other properties, from vacant lots to a 76-unit apartment building. I have never been faced with that scenario. If I were to face that scenario, I know without a doubt that I would deal with the occupants better than a bank. They do not deal with the occupants, they just send out the sheriff to evict.

Consider the Alternative

If the bank or another investor gets the property, they may not show sympathy or compassion. They may not even care about trying to make the transition a smooth one for the occupant. Some do not want to bother themselves with talking to the occupant; they just let the sheriff go out and put them on the street. Worse yet, some may take advantage of them by scaming what little money they have away from them. I have heard about a scam many times from those who have already been taken advantage of during all phases of the foreclosure process. A so-called investor tells the people that he can get the occupants financing to save their home. They charge a $200 up to $1000 application fee up front. Of course, the desperate people pay it. Then they never hear from that person again. The good Lord in his wisdom will see to it that these scam artists get their just reward some day!

The bottom line is that I know that problems with people losing their homes to foreclosure exist. Someone is going to profit from it, and it might as well be someone like me who is going to take an unavoidable negative situation for someone else and take the most positive action available and sometimes even be compensated for the effort. That is certainly reasonable, and the people are better off because of my involvement.

There are some situations where I actually help people save their homes by doing some counseling with them, and I make nothing on it. Sometimes it is just a matter of lifting a heavy burden from their shoulders by answering their questions about how the whole foreclosure process works. There are other situations where I assist people with refinancing or selling their homes to save their equity. It all depends on the circumstances. See Case in Point # 22, Midlothian.

Communicating with the Occupant

Once I have acquired a property via the auction, I always approach the occupants as a middleman person — a manager for the new owner / investor. It seems to be an easier approach; people are less intimidated. I even go so far as getting business cards and using a d/b/a (doing business as) Property Management Services. It also is wise to remember that their emotions may be sensitive. Use a low aggressive approach; you will get more cooperation with honey than you will with vinegar.

Sometimes the occupant is not the owner at all, he is a tenant who has been paying rent for the last twelve plus months. Once in a while the occupant is a "Contract for Deed" buyer, which means he gave the owner a down payment and the owner financed the balance. Then while the contract buyer was making monthly mortgage payments to the owner, the owner was not making monthly mortgage payments to the bank / mortgage company. Either the buyer did not use an attorney, or the attorney was incompetent in protecting the buyer against this occurrence.

It has always been a part of my procedure to communicate with the occupants to make the transition as smooth as possible and to make an effort to help them with a new beginning. Sometimes this involves keeping them on as tenants, paying their first month's rent and security deposit, or just giving them $100 - $500 for the keys and possession. The most important point to remember about all this is that an ex-owner has developed a very bad habit of not paying anything for many months for his home. I saw one case where it had been five years. There was a bankruptcy involved, and the mortgage had been sold in a bulk sale, slowing up the process. **You never give them anything until they give you the keys and possession.** Otherwise, something will always come up to prevent them from moving. The house or apartment they had lined up is not ready; they could not get a truck; the dog died; etc.

Reasons for Foreclosure

The first thing to understand is that every deal, every situation, is different. From my experience one of the major reasons for foreclosure is divorce.

- **Divorce:** See Case in Point # 3, Forestville. One spouse leaves the other, and with the loss of that spouse's income the remaining spouse can no longer pay the mortgage. Sensible people will of course recognize the reality of the circumstances and either take a boarder or sell before losing the house. However, having human weaknesses as some of us do, especially when emotions are involved in the equation, the spouse with the house sometimes wants to show the other that he / she can hold on to the house. Or, that the other should pay the mortgage, and therefore refuses to do so. You would think that when they have equity in their home, they would reason with one another enough to at least sell their home and split the equity. However, this is not the case when emotional contempt plays a role. Neither one wants to see the other get anything. Eventually, they both get nothing.

My mentor used to tell a story about a friend of his who saw an ad in the newspaper for a Cadillac for sale for $25. He thought it must have been a typing error, but even $2500 was a good price. He dialed the number, and a woman answered. He mentioned the ad and that it said $25. She said, *"That's right."* He chuckled and asked, *"Does it have tires? Does it have an engine?"* She assured him it ran perfectly well. He made an appointment, went over, and bought it. Before leaving, he could not help but to ask, *"Why did you sell me this Cadillac for only $25?"* She said, *"My husband recently died after thirty five years of marriage. It turned out that he had a mistress and in his will he left her the Cadillac or the proceeds from the sale of the Cadillac!"*

Infidelity probably plays a major role in foreclosure situations. People in foreclosure are in emotional turmoil! They are on an emotional roller coaster with up's and downs.

There are many more reasons why people go into foreclosure.

- **Death:** This is a big one. People die and stop paying their mortgage. I have bought several homes where the previous owner had died. Now, logical thinking would say that the heirs would take care of the problem.

Most of the time that is probably so. However, I bought one where the heirs could not agree on anything, especially who would be responsible to pay the mortgage. See Case in Point # 23, Markham. Sometimes heirs do not exist, or they live out of state and are unable to deal with it, even when there is much equity to be had. See Case in Point # 18, Desplaines. Death of a spouse sometimes paralyzes the remaining spouse from taking care of his or her bills, especially if the deceased spouse always took care of it, or if there is no family or good friends around to get involved in helping out. See Case in Point # 12, Evergreen Park.

- **Alcoholism and Drugs**: Addictions are the cause of much heart ache. I have heard stories from one spouse about how the other spouse was spending their mortgage payments on cocaine. Substance abuse and addiction seem to distort a person's sense of reality and logical thinking. These people are in a state of denial probably about every area of their lives — not just the foreclosure on their home. I have tried talking with these people to help them avoid an eviction, offering cash and other help, and consulting with other extended family members. Generally losing their home, being evicted, and hitting rock bottom is part of the process for them to face reality, so they can start the climb back up. See Case in Point # 15, Dickens.

- **Job Loss:** Personally, in my early days I was married with one child and I found myself between jobs and out of money. I resorted to doing what I did as a teenager. I knocked on doors to mow or rake yards or perform odd jobs for money. However, some people just become paralyzed unless they can find a job equal to what they had or better. They just spiral down until someone kicks them in the butt or they hit bottom.

- **Gambling:** As I write this I am currently taking possession of a nice split level home in Alsip, Illinois. One of my lender clients recently got the deed on it. I talked with an adult daughter of the owners who lost the home. Both are doctors making an excellent income. Their problem? The lure — casino river boats. These floating dens of iniquity are a scourge on society. I realize some people may think that a harsh statement. However, when you seriously think about it, casinos only exist for being able to prey on the weak and provide entertainment for some of the wealthy. The problem is that the weak make up the majority. If that was not so, they would not be in business. See Case in Point # 22, Midlothian.

- **Medical Problems:** Some people lack the ability to acquire, or just do not want to pay for, adequate insurance. When a major medical problem arises, they pour all their financial resources into taking care of their loved one and put off paying the mortgage payments. They rationalize, "*I'll catch it up later.*" See Case in Point # 6, Hickory Hills.

- **Running from the Law or in Jail:** It is hard to keep up payments when someone is on the run or incarcerated. See Case in Point # 1, Harlem Ave, and # 20, Wentworth.

- **Job Transfer:** People transfer and cannot keep up two payments. See Case in Point # 24, Sauk Village.

- **Business Loss:** Some people believe working real hard and putting everything they have into their business, including their mortgage payments, will make it a success. Sometimes it works! Other times it does not. The list goes on and on, but I think you get the point by now.

Do not make the mistake of thinking that you need to know it all before you start approaching people. If you think this way, you will never buy anything. This book will provide you the necessary foundation, and it will familiarize you with the procedures and techniques. However, for the knowledge to really sink in, you just need to get out there and start the process. That is where the real learning takes place.

Just Do It!

CHAPTER 2

The Foreclosure Process

Different States have different means by which to accomplish a foreclosure.

Lien **Judicial**	**Trust** **Deed** **Lien** **Judicial**	**Mortgage** **Intermediate** **P.O.S.***
Florida		Arkansas
Indiana		Massachusetts
Iowa	Arizona	
Kansas		
Kentucky	**Mortgage**	**Mortgage**
Louisiana	**Intermediate**	**Title**
Montana	**Strict Foreclosure**	**P.O.S.***
Nebraska		
New Mexico	Connecticut	Alabama
New York	Vermont	Rhode Island
North Dakota	**Mortgage**	New Hampshire
Oklahoma	**Intermediate**	
South Carolina	**Judicial**	
Utah		
Washington	Delaware	
	Illinois	
	New Jersey	
	Ohio	

Trust Deed **Lien** **P.O.S.***	**Mortgage** **Title** **Judicial**	**Mortgage** **Lien** **P.O.S.***
Alaska California Colorado Idaho Oregon Texas **Trust Deed** **Lien** **P.O.S.*** Hawaii Maryland Tennessee	Pennsylvania **Trust Deed Intermediate P.O.S.*** Washington D.C. Mississippi North Carolina Virginia West Virginia	Michigan Minnesota Nevada South Dakota Wisconsin Wyoming

* Power Of Sale

I feel it is necessary to provide definitions of some specific terms at this point.

Trustee's Deed

This is a conveyance of title from a trust to another party.

The grantor is the trust, through its fiduciary or agent, called a trustee. The trustee acts only upon written direction of the beneficiaries of the trust.

If you take out a trust deed, you are called the grantor or trustor. The third party appointed by the lender to hold the trust deed in trust is called the trustee. The lender is called the beneficiary. This trust deed is a security instrument, not to be confused with other types of trusts.

Note and Mortgage

A mortgage consists of two parts; the note, which is considered to be evidence of the debt, and the mortgage contract, which secures the debt. The note is a promise to repay the loan. While in the mortgage the borrower agrees to be subject to certain legal action if he does not repay the loan as promised. If you take out a mortgage on a property, you are called the mortgagor because you give a mortgage to the lender to whom you owe money. The lender is called the mortgagee.

Security Deed

In Georgia, the only state with a security deed to secure a loan on real estate, you are called the grantor and the lender is called the grantee. As a grantor under the terms of the security deed, you have only an equitable interest in the property until the debt is paid. According to Georgia law, a mortgage is a mere lien, while a security deed actually passes title to property. v

Lien versus Title

A mortgage or trust deed is a contract, and the laws pertaining to contracts generally apply. In some states a mortgage is really a transfer or conveyance of real estate, upon condition, as security for the payment of a debt. That is why those states using this form of mortgage or trust deed conveyance are called *"Title Theory States"* because the instrument actually conveys title.

In other states a mortgage is considered and treated only as a lien. A lien is a hold claim, which one person has on the property of another as security for some debt.

A lien is an encumbrance. (see the glossary) A person purchasing real estate encumbered by a mortgage takes the property subject to a lien. Liens also include judgments recorded against the property and unpaid taxes.

Power of Sale

One of the features that most trust deeds incorporate is a power of sale. There is very little difference between a mortgage and a trust deed unless a default occurs and a foreclosure is initiated.

Typically under a power of sale foreclosure the trustee sends a letter informing the grantor or property owner that he has not paid the note payments due and demands immediate payment. If the payment is not received within a couple of weeks, the trustee sends another letter informing the owner that the loan has been accelerated and again demands immediate payment. After a statutory period of time, about four weeks, during which time the property is advertised, the property is sold at public auction.

Various Methods of Foreclosure Nationwide

The most important asset foreclosure investors can have is a thorough knowledge of their state's foreclosure procedures. To attempt to provide such detail would require a separate book, therefore I will only touch upon some general procedures and specific information for the states of Illinois and California. Other states are similar. However, you need to do some research for specific procedures. Statutes and procedures vary from state to state. The information provided herein is for informational purposes and may not be 100% accurate in your particular area.

Also, laws change from time to time. Therefore, it is prudent and advisable to check and verify current laws and procedures in your area. Chapter Three instructs you on how to go about getting specific information for your area.

The prime requirement in most states is that there be an orderly process by which the grantor or mortgagor is given a final opportunity to cure the default. If the default is not remedied, then there must be an equitable procedure by which the property is exposed to public sale in such a manner as to yield its best price. The objective and the result are the same, no matter whether the sale is judicial or by power of sale.

Generally speaking, the breach of any obligation of the grantor or mortgagor under the security instrument will create a default. This would include failure to pay insurance premiums. In addition to the lender looking at the ability of the borrower to repay the loan, the lender has the right to ensure that the collateral for the mortgage (the property) remains in good condition and free of property tax liens.

Mortgage versus Trust Deed Foreclosure

The difference in the security instruments only becomes important in the event of a default. As for the borrower, he can lose his property very quickly if he has signed over a trust deed or security deed with power of sale. If he has given a mortgage or trust deed which can be foreclosed by judicial process, he has more time to work out a solution. This is due to the nature of the judicial process. The foreclosure proceeds through various stages to the sale.

There are all sorts of differences in statutes from state to state regarding foreclosure. In Michigan, for example, a mortgage, which creates a lien on property is generally sold by power-of-sale procedures. In Florida and Illinois, however, a mortgage foreclosure is judicial.

The Judicial Process

The First Stage — Filing of the Lis Pendens

As I am familiar with it in the state of Illinois

When a lender begins the foreclosure process, the borrower is usually a minimum of three months in arrears. You can be assured by this time that late notices and a thirty day demand and acceleration letter has been sent. Most lenders file the Complaint of Foreclosure lawsuit (lis pendens) at that point. However, I have seen where an individual was 15 months in arrears, and the lender still had not filed. Keep in mind that things do not always work like clockwork for lenders. They experience problems, too. This is true especially when they have a large number of delinquencies and / or a big turn over of employees. Some lenders sell or buy millions of dollars worth of loans in bulk packages. Imagine all the paper work. Do you suppose it is possible that occasionally a file is mis-placed? In Cook County, Illinois, which covers the city of Chicago and some suburbs, there are between four hundred and six hundred new foreclosure cases filed every month. Eighty to one hundred sixty go to auction every week. Therefore, there are literally thousands of people in foreclosure at any given point in time. Throughout the country there are literally millions!

Once a foreclosure case has been filed, the attorneys for the lender must publish a legal notice announcing the filing of the lawsuit in a paper of general circulation for three consecutive weeks. Diligent efforts must be made by the attorney for the lender to serve the home owner and other parties of record who may have an interest in the subject property, a summons notifying them of the lawsuit and to file an answer. (This is only accomplished through public notice in the newspaper if the lender is unable to locate the defendants.) The summons also gives the home owner a date by which he has the right to file an answer to the lawsuit or appear in court on the assigned date to answer, generally thirty days. Most people do not even bother filing an answer or appearing in court. Keep in mind that one has to go downtown to the county court house during working hours and pay a fee to file. The few who do find it to be of no use because there is no good legal reason for not making mortgage payments. A good reason for filing an answer to the lawsuit would be if a rule or law in regards to lending practices has been violated (regulation Z), which is rare.

The Second Stage

Order of Judgment and Order for Sale

After all the defendants have been served with the summons and if no defendant has filed an answer to the complaint, or after the answer has been heard and dismissed, then the lender's attorney can move the court to enter a default Judgement. The Judge examines the file and the pleadings and will enter Judgement against all who have been served. If any defendants filed a response to the complaint then the attorney must reply with appropriate pleadings. This may take some time depending upon the circumstances however, ultimately the case is brought to Judgement.

After the Judgment of Foreclosure and Order for Sale is granted, the lender has the right to refuse reinstatement of the loan and demand full payoff. However, occasionally lenders allow a loan to be reinstated just prior to the auction.

Redemption Period

After entry of the Judgement, the statutory period of redemption runs. This is the interval of time within which the defendants may pay off the entire mortgage debt and regain their full rights in the property. If the property can be shown to the Court to be abandoned and that defendants have no intention of returning, the redemption period can be shortened. In the normal cases, however, the redemption period runs to the later date of: seven months from when the last of the mortgagors were served or three months from the date of entry of Judgement.

The Third Stage — The Auction

Although auctions are held by different entities, the procedures are basically the same. The auction date notice is published in a paper of general circulation once per week for three consecutive weeks. The auction itself is actually less formal than one would expect. It is not uncommon for them to be conducted in a hallway or small, out-of-the-way room. Unlike HUD and VA auctions, which require bids to be submitted in a sealed envelope or electronically (privately) per the internet, this is an open bidding forum. Personally I prefer this method, because you have more opportunity for a better deal and you know immediately if you won the bid.

The Sheriff Deputy or other person conducting the sale will call out the case number, the address and say, *"Plaintiff, what is your bid?"* The attorney or law clerk will then announce the amount owed the lender to the penny. The auctioneer then says, *"Are there any other bids?"* Then any interested person can bid above that amount. I recommend bidding one dollar more. If someone else is there, then the bidding escalates by a minimum of $100 increments or more. As a general practice, some auctioneers will require $1,000 increments. There are no hard and fast rules; however, that is what is encouraged. If no bids, or after the last bid, the auctioneer says, *"Once, twice, thrice, sold!"*

I have won many at a dollar more; I have gotten some after a bidding contest; and I have lost many more. It is like anything else; it is a numbers game. The more often you are there to bid, the more you will lose, and the more you will win.

In the five counties surrounding the Chicago Illinois area, ten percent of the bid amount is required in certified funds or money order immediately following the auction. The balance within twenty four hours. Of course, winning the bid feels great! However, it is not a positive experience for long if you have not done your homework. Study Chapter Three on Research. Buying a junior mortgage when you thought it was a first, can be costly. I have seen investors become caught up in the frenzy of bidding and pay too much for a property.

Be prepared to be asked at the beginning of your bid to show your deposit check. People have been known to bid without deposit money with them. This, of course, is not fair when competing with someone who does have it. When competing for thousands of dollars of literally instant profit, it is very serious; it can be very tense!

You get a simple receipt for your cash payments. Within a few more days you can pick up your Certificate of Sale, which is simply a document that acknowledges you as the successful bidder. Within a week to thirty days, depending on the Judge's calendar, a representative from the lender's attorneys' office sets a motion before the Judge to move the court for an order approving the sale. The Judge must examine the sale documents and compare them to the Judgement. The Judge also examines any request for a deficiency Judgement and must approve the amount. Included in the motion is also an Order for Possession which is placed with the sheriff, if necessary, to accomplish the eviction. The Order for Possession is automatically stayed thirty days from the approval of the sale if the defendants are still in the premises. The deed is issued by the entity that conducted the sale.

Sheriff's Sale

If it is a sheriff's sale auction, the sheriff will call out the sheriff's sale number, then the address. The sheriffs department, works in conjunction with the local county and city government.

The sales have been held Tuesday, Wednesday, and Thursday at 12 noon.

Until 1992 they were the only entity conducting the foreclosure auctions except for the Commissioner's Sale.

Commissioners Sale

A Commissioner's Sale is one held by the federal government because one of the parties to the lawsuit is out of state. However, this appears to be optional because I have known of Sheriff Sales involving out-of-state lenders. An attorney with certain legal standing is appointed to be a commissioner and conducts the sale. (location, etc. per the legal notice).

Private Entities

Certain individuals have taken the legal procedures necessary to put themselves in the position of conducting foreclosure auctions. What at one time appeared to be a monopoly of the Sheriff's Department is now open to free enterprise. Inter-County Judicial Sales, Judicial Sales Corporation, and Kallen Financial are the names of three such entities operating out of the Chicago area.

Intercounty Sales Corporation
Cook County - 120 W. Madison #718A, Chicago; 11:00 AM
Lake County - 5465 Grand Ave. #100, Gurnee; 9:00 AM
Dupage County - 755 S. Naperville Road, Wheaton; 9:00 AM
For all Information - 312-444-1122

Judicial Sales Corporation
Cook County - 33 N. Dearborn #201, Chicago; 10:30 AM
Lake County - 18 N. County, Waukegan; 9:00 or 11:00 AM
Dupage County - 505 N. County Farm Road, Wheaton; 1:00 PM
Kane County - 100 3rd Third Street, Geneva; 1:00 PM
Will County - 14 Jefferson Street, Joliet; 1:00 PM
For All Information - 312-236-7253

Sheriff's Sale
Cook County - 7th Floor outside room 701, Richard J. Daley Center, Chicago 312-603-3341; 12:00 Noon
Lake County - Conference Room, Justice Center, 25 S. Utica Street, Waukegan 847-360-6300; 9:00 AM
Dupage County - Main Lobby 501 N. County Farm Rd., Wheaton 708-682-7250; 10:00AM
Kane County - Room 110 Kane County Courthouse 100 S. third Street, Geneva 630-208-2010; 9:00 AM
Will County - 14 W. Jefferson, Main Floor Hallway, Joliet 815-727-8400; 11:00 AM
McHenry County - 220 N. Seminary, Room C240, Woodstock 815-334-4242; 10:00 AM

Kallen Financial
Cook County - 118 N. Clark Room 120, Chicago 312-643-1903; 11:30 AM

The Fourth Stage

Most properties that go to auction for substantially less than value will be bought by an investor or home buyer. Occasionally one slips through the cracks, and the lender ends up with it. In the Chicago-Cook County area less than twenty percent of the eighty to one hundred sixty properties that go to auction each week actually are bought. This is primarily due to the first mortgage indebtedness being near or above the value of the real estate. With no one bidding on the property it goes to the plaintiff or lender. It is now considered an R.E.O. If the property was insured by F.H.A. or V.A. it now becomes a H.U.D. or V.A. property. I discuss this further in Chapter Three and Six.

Sometimes a property may be over-indebted with several liens. However, if the debt of the first mortgage (or even the first and second mortgage debt total) is low enough compared to the value, it can still be worthwhile to buy. See Case in Point # 9, Foster Ave. Keep in mind that if the second mortgage or junior liens do not bid in at the auction, their debt is wiped out — cleansed from the property. *"Why wouldn't junior lien holders represent themselves and protect their interest in the property?"* You may be thinking. Well, to bid in at the auction, a junior lien (any lien other than the first) simply bids above the opening bid. If they win, they are responsible to pay off all liens that are superior to them. If it is a second mortgage opening the bid, then they are still responsible to pay off the first mortgage. Therefore, a person in a junior lien position may not be prepared financially to pay off superior liens and prefer or have no choice but to just walk away.

The Trustee Sale Process
As carried out in California

Names of the people involved in the Foreclosure Process are the Trustor, the Beneficiary, and the Trustee. The Trustor is the borrower of the loan who pledges the property as security for the loan by a Trust Deed. He is the property owner. The Beneficiary is the lender to the trustor. The Trustee is a third party who represents the beneficiary and will foreclose upon the beneficiary's orders.

Step 1: In the beginning the owner stops making his trust deed payments. The lender may allow these payments not to be made for many months before he starts the foreclosure action. However, he must wait a minimum of ten days beyond the due date of the monthly payment before he can file a notice of default.

Before the notice of default is filed, the note payments may be several months behind. This is not foreclosure. They are just "slow pays" or "non-performing loans."

If an investor buys a property prior to the notice of default being filed, he will not have to comply with any foreclosure laws. These laws only apply once the notice of default has been recorded. They specify the type of contract the investor must have with the seller, the seller's rights, and the rights of other parties. The investor can make any type of contract prior to the notice of default being recorded.

Step 2: Once the loan is more than ten days past due, the lender can ask his trustee to record a notice of default. When this notice is recorded with the county recorder, it starts a three-month time period. During this three-month period, the property owner is told in the notice how much money it will take to make up the missed payments, late charges, trustee's fees, and other charges necessary to cure or reinstate the loan at the old interest rate and terms. Because of interest being charged, the amount to cure becomes larger every day.

If the property owner pays that total amount due, the lender will ask the trustee to record a notice of rescission with the county recorder. The missed payments and other charges have been paid and the property is no longer in foreclosure. The loan has been reinstated at the old interest rate and terms.

The trustee must mail by certified mail or registered mail a copy of the notice of default to the trustor or owner of the property within ten days of recording. The trustee must also mail copies of the notice of default within ten days of recording to all those persons who have filed a request to be notified of any default.

The Reality of Real Estate Investing

Within thirty days of the recording of a notice of default, a copy of the notice must be sent by registered or certified mail to the following persons, whether of not they have recorded a request for notice:

A. The new owner of the property if the original trustor has sold the property before the notice of default was recorded.

B. Any lenders or beneficiaries under trust deeds recorded after the trust deed is in default and being foreclosed on. For example, if there are three loans on a property and the lender on the first loan has not been getting paid, he records a notice of default; he must send a notice to the beneficiaries on the second and third loans on the property, letting them know that he is foreclosing on the property.

C. The assignees of any interests of the beneficiaries described in B above, and various other persons also entitled to notice.

The beneficiary or trustee must accept payment from the trustor or borrower or new owner of the property during this three-month period and reinstate the loan at the old interest rate and terms. They do not have to accept partial payments.

If the owner or a past owner files bankruptcy while the property is in foreclosure, the foreclosure process cannot proceed until the bankruptcy court releases it. This may take from one month to a year or more.

Sometimes it is possible to negotiate with the lender to extend the three-month period, but usually the owner and lender are not communicating.

Step 3: After the three-month reinstatement period is over and the payments have not been brought current, the trustee can then file a notice of sale with the county recorder and publish it once a week over a period of at least 21 days in a newspaper of general circulation. A newspaper of general circulation can mean almost any local paper, including newspapers targeted for lawyers.

The notice of sale is mailed by the trustee to those requesting it and to the trustor or homeowner and to all those persons described earlier who have a right to receive the notice of default. The Trustee must mail the notice of sale to these persons within 10 days of recording the notice of sale.

A notice of trustee's sale must contain certain information. It must state the date, time, and place of the trustee's sale, the address, description of the property to be sold, the name and address of the beneficiary. It must state the total amount of the unpaid loan secured by the trust deed plus the reasonable estimated costs, expenses, and advances as of the date of the first publication of the notice of sale. The notice of sale must have the trustee's name, address, and telephone number. You can tell from the notice of sale how much will be needed in cash or cashier's check to bid at the auction.

The trustee must hold the sale in the county where the property is located. The sale must take place on a business day between the hours of 9:00 A.M. and 5:00 P.M. The trustee may postpone the sale by announcing it at the time specified in the notice of sale. The trustee, at his discretion or upon notice from the beneficiary, has the right to postpone the sale three times. If he postpones the sale a fourth time, he must again publish a notice of sale in the newspaper over a period of twenty one days.

Step 4: Before the bidding begins at the trustee's sale, each bidder must show evidence to the trustee of his ability to bid. The bidder must qualify with the trustee by showing the trustee either cash or a cashier's check or other forms of proof acceptable to the trustee.

After the sale the successful bidder must immediately give the full bidding price to the trustee. Each bid at the sale is an irrevocable offer. Failure of the winning bidder to deposit the full cash price makes the bidder liable for damages which the trustee may sustain, including attorney's fees and court costs. Failure of the bidder to deposit the money upon a winning bid is also a misdemeanor, punishable by a fine of up to $2,500.

There are several laws designed to stop practices of offering or accepting a proposition not to bid against one another. They are punishable by one year in jail and a $10,000 fine.

The only bidders who do not have to bring cash or cashier's check to the trustee's sale are the beneficiaries of the trust deed which is foreclosing on the property. They are entitled to a "credit bid" the amount of the loan and fees and costs due them. If the bidding is higher than the amount stated in the notice of sale, the excess of the bid will go to pay the expenses of sale and then to junior lien holders who are beneficiaries of trust deed records after the trust deed whose sale this is.

In the event there is excess money left over after all loans recorded against the property have been paid, the owner will get that excess.

After the trustee's sale, a trustee's deed will be issued to the successful bidder. The deed does not guarantee clear title to the bidder. The purchaser takes title subject to superior loans and rights recorded before the trust deed sale was recorded. That is why it is prudent on the part of the purchaser to do his homework. He needs to know that the trust deed he is purchasing is in first position or that with any superior liens it is still a good investment.

The Home Equity Sales Law

In 1979 some new laws were passed protecting the rights of homeowners in foreclosure. These laws require the purchaser to fill out a home equity sales contract. This contract dictates the terms and conditions under which a homeowner can sell his property and the type of contract to be used in such sale. These laws apply only to a property being used as the personal residence of the owner. The property may be a single family home, a condo, or a two-to-four unit apartment building.

This law provides that the seller has five business days in which to rescind the contract.

The Home Equity Sales Law does not apply to the following:

1. Any residential property that is not occupied by the owner.
2. Any commercial property.
3. Any raw land.
4. Any industrial property.
5. Any residential property of five units or more.
6. A sale to a blood relative of a seller or a seller's spouse.
7. Any property which the purchaser intends to occupy as his residence after the purchase.
8. A purchaser at a trustee's sale.
9. A beneficiary under a trust deed on the property.
10. Any property where the foreclosure process has not begun because no notice of default has been recorded.

If the Home Equity Sales Law is not complied with, the seller may reclaim his property within two years. Failure of the purchaser to use an equity purchase agreement under those circumstances which the laws state it is necessary will enable the seller to sue the buyer for damages, set aside the sale within a two-year time period, and receive attorney's fees and court costs. Also, a violation of these laws can result in criminal penalties which include fines and jail.

Title companies are reluctant to issue a policy of title insurance unless it is clear that the purchase price and money paid to the seller, while below market value, was at least fair.

How to Read Default Notices

- **SITUS**: The address of the property being foreclosed.
- **LEGAL**: The "legal description" pertains to subdivision maps at the county recorder's office. It corresponds to the street address in "SITUS."
- **TRUSTOR**: The borrower of the loan in default. Usually, it is the current owner / occupant of a single family house. However, the property may have

been sold by the original trustor after the loan was recorded. In this case the new owner's name is not readily available.
- **ADDRESS:** Can be the trustor's old address when he bought the property described under "SITUS," or it can be the trustor's current address if he is a landlord renting out the situs.
- **ASSESSED:** These are the county tax collector's assessed values for taxing purposes. Do not use these figures as a basis for estimating the current value of the property. "L" stands for the land value and "I" stands for the value of the improvements on the property (i.e. house, buildings etc.) If you add the two figures together and multiply by four, you will get the current value of the property. The property is worth at least that much, perhaps more. Check actual recent sales to be more accurate.
- **TRUST DEED AMOUNT:** The original amount of the loan secured by the Trust Deed on the property.
- **DATE:** The date the Trust Deed (loan) was recorded.
- **PRINCIPAL INTEREST DUE:** The amount of missed payments owed as of the date stated, including principal and interest.
- **DEFAULT:** The date the Notice of Default was recorded. This starts the three-month reinstatement period running.
- **TRUSTEE:** The person or firm conducting the foreclosure process. The number following the trustee's name is the file number. If you call them inquiring about the property, they will need this number to answer your questions.
- **BENEFICIARY:** The lender on the loan in default. It is possible to make a deal with the beneficiary depending upon whether the beneficiary is a private lender (former owner), F.H.A. lender, conventional lender, etc.

IMPORTANT

Each default listing is for <u>one loan only</u>. There may be more than one loan on the property. As each trustee records a notice of default for his beneficiary, the notice is published by one of the services. The same property may appear over and over again.

You cannot determine the equity from this one default listing, and even the figure listed may not be accurate. It is merely a starting point.

The information provided herein is a valuable starting point.

Remember that over time some laws, procedures, and locations can change.

Always be willing to ask questions. Keep in my the peopleworking in the court houses are paid hourly and will be there the same amount of time whether or not they answer questions for you. Most are more than happy to share their knowledge with you. It makes them feel important. So never shy away from aggressive information seeking. Its called research.

CHAPTER 3

Research

Lead Gathering

Now that you have a basic understanding of what foreclosures are all about, the question you need answered is: How and where do I get the information on properties in foreclosure? Below are the sources:

- **Legal notices**
- **County court house**
- **Private entities**
- **Banks or lending institutions**
- **HUD or VA**
- **Realtors**

Legal Notices

You should remember I have mentioned in Chapter Two that legal notices are published in newspapers of general circulation for three consecutive weeks. This is done twice — first upon the filing of the foreclosure case, and second prior to the foreclosure auction.

These legal notices can serve as initial leads. You can decide based on the address if you want to follow up. Sometimes there is also a balance owed or judgment amount listed. Therefore, you have an idea about how much is owed. However, it is up to the attorney's discretion whether or not to include this amount. If you live near a big city, another newspaper where the greatest number of notices are published would be a legal newspaper. In the Chicago, Illinois, area it is called the "Law Bulletin."

County Court House

A foreclosure is basically a lawsuit. The lender or plaintiff is suing the property owner or defendant. Lawsuits are of public record and therefore available to anyone who may wish to look at the information.

You can find the files on properties in foreclosure usually in the county court house building. It is just a matter of going and asking, *"Where is the department that has the files on properties in foreclosure?"* In Chicago it is the eighth floor of the Daley Center. These case files are assigned a number and typically filed in chronological order. This number is listed in the legal notices. Therefore, you can arrive at the court house with some specific numbers to look up, or ask the clerk for the last case file for that day. Some counties keep a log book of the new cases filed and will make that available to you to choose which case numbers you want to pull. Armed with that case number, you can request other file numbers previous to that one or afterwards on your next trip to the court house.

Now that you have the file in your hands, what do you do with it? Usually there is a small area with a table and chairs. Sit there and begin to thumb through the file. On your first time it is probably a good idea to read through the entire file and become familiar with everything that is there. After that, you scan through the documents for specific information.

The file includes:

- **Complaint of Foreclosure**
- **Summons**
- **Judgment of Foreclosure and Sale**
- **and various other documents**

The Complaint of Foreclosure

Some of the useful information you will find here includes the plaintiff's and defendant's names, original date of the mortgage, and original amount. The older the mortgage, the more the loan balance has been paid down and the more possibility for equity and appreciation. The principal balance, amount of back payments, monthly payments, and interest rate can also be found here. Other lien holders are usually mentioned here. Sometimes a copy of the mortgage note may be attached to this document which would show the type of mortgage being foreclosed (VA, FHA, or Conventional). Evaluating this information helps you determine if further research or a drive-by is warranted.

The Summons

This is a copy of the official notice showing service of the Complaint of Foreclosure by the sheriff upon the defendants of the foreclosure lawsuit. Some useful information sometimes found here is who was served a summons and where, a brief description of the property, and if it is vacant. A list of other defendants served can also be found here. This would include any liens of record or individuals whose names appear on the title. When the attorneys for the bank check the title on a property, everyone with a lien or interest in the property must be served notice of the pending foreclosure lawsuit.

Private Entities

I first became involved in this business in the early 1980's with a man named Gary Furstenfeld. Already very successful in buying foreclosures and bank owned properties, he quickly became my mentor. He, of course, was quite familiar with how tedious the task is of researching the court files. An idea was born! That idea is known as "The Foreclosure Directory." It provides the main information that a prospective investor looks for in beginning his research:

Full Address City & Zip Property Type	Owner's Name Service Address	Lender's Name Attorney & Phone #	Original Debt Year/Mtg Typ Interest rate Document #	Balance Due Per Diem % Date Calculation

Case # Prior Mortgages	Subsequent Encumbrances	Sheriff Sale # & sale date P.I.N. #

This information is researched and organized into a directory, thus saving the investor much time. Time is money! There is a section for the current foreclosure cases filed. These you deal directly with the owners. Then there is a section for the cases approaching the auction. These directories usually cover one or more counties, and are generally sold on a yearly subscription basis. The Directory can be found in most large cities. For Chicago the service covers the five-county Chicago-land area. If one is available in your area, I recommend utilizing a publication like this because time is money, and this saves much time. More information is available and ordering can be done via my Web Site.

www.HomeBargains.com

Banks / Lending Institutions

Of course, you can contact lenders directly for properties they have foreclosed on and now own, R.E.O.'s. (I discuss in Chapter Six how to approach them.) You may be wondering, "If bank owned properties are good deals, why are they not sold through the foreclosure process or at the auction?" I will tell you. Some people in the foreclosure process just will not cooperate. Imagine that! (This is discussed further in Chapters Four and Five.) Some properties simply have too much debt compared to value to be bought at the auction. The lenders usually bid in what they are owed to the penny, regardless of value. I have seen where a lender has bid less than what they were owed, apparently in an effort to stimulate a bid. However, they usually do not advertise this fact ahead of time, and therefore, no one is usually prepared. Keep in mind nothing is ever 100%. My point is that lenders must realize sooner or later that the debt on a given property is irrelevant to what it can sell for.

They really could take more advantage of the auction if they used their minds or simply cared more. You see, the bank representatives, until they experience the losses due to poor strategy and judgment of reality, make poor decisions on behalf of their employer. Also realize they have to have incentive to care, if they do not do so naturally, about losing dollars for their employer. If $10,000 - $20,000 is lost, their weekly pay check is not affected. Of course, in time if they do not wise up, their job security will be at risk.

Some properties that have low debt compared to value sometimes also end up owned by the bank. They simply fall through the cracks. I have bid and lost on many more properties than the ones I have won. With some of the ones I have won, I was the only bidder and therefore got the property for $1 more than what was owed. If I had not followed up on that particular property, the bank would have become the owner. Remember the phrase, *"There is always room for one more."* No one hundred people can ever cover it all. Case in Point # 8 Rockwell.

HUD And VA
(Housing Urban Development and Veterans Administration)

These are federally insured loans — FHA (Federal Housing Authority) and VA. Basically these programs insure the lender for making low down payment loans (FHA - 3%; VA - no down payment) against losses in the event of default. Once these properties go through the foreclosure process, HUD and VA take the responsibility to sell the property. HUD and VA properties are listed in newspapers with a large circulation. HUD also has a web site, a link to that site can be found on the hot links page on my web site. **www.HomeBargains.com**

I personally do not pursue HUD and VA properties. Although I have heard of people who knew someone that made money on HUD and VA properties, I never did. Oh, I tried, but there was always someone willing to pay more, and more often than not it seemed to me that they paid too much. Also, it is a sealed bid process. I prefer the open bid process at the foreclosure auctions. I can never keep up with all the leads as it is, and I feel the open bid process is where the highest possible profits are made.

Realtors

Realtors can also be a valuable resource. Banks will list their properties with them. They also have other motivated seller situations available to them, such as handyman specials, divorce, etc. Let them know of your seriousness. Tell them that you are a cash buyer and that you can close in two to three weeks, even if you do not personally have the cash. As long as you have a resource to get it, that is all that matters. Offering to pay the Realtors a buyer's commission ($2,000 flat fee) in addition to what they will get from the seller can be worthwhile. This would be contingent upon the deal being profitable enough to justify it, of course. If you do not feel it is, then you negotiate it for a lesser fee or out all together. For example, a $30,000 investment should return to you at least $10,000 in profit after paying the buyer's commission. This should give the realtor incentive to help you locate and negotiate good deals. Typically on a $30,000 deal the Realtor will only get $450 after splitting with his broker. If he is the broker / owner, then it is $900. If the property is their listing also, then it is $1,800, typically. This still may not be enough incentive to work hard for you. It is like dangling the apple in front of the horse, you will get more deals coming your way.

The Analysis / Pinpoint the Numbers

Once you have decided on a specific property to pursue, it becomes necessary to pinpoint the numbers involved.

Acquisition Cost

This is the amount of money you are willing to spend to acquire the property. There are also the miscellaneous fees associated with that acquisition, such as title charges, recording of the deed, attorney fees, professional inspection, water bills, back and current taxes, etc.

Holding Cost

This includes property insurance, taxes, utilities, lawn maintenance, snow removal, etc. Do not forget the interest on the money you are using for all of this. You calculate this cost as a recurring monthly cost, even though you pay the insurance for a year at a time. You do get a refund of the unused amount once you sell. Realtors can provide you with the average market time for the area so that you know how many months to estimate. You should be able to sell quicker than the average time due to your property being newly remodeled and available for immediate occupancy. However, calculate your market time at least a month longer than the average for the area to play it safe.

Remodeling Cost

This, of course, is your cost to fix the property. Chapters Ten and Eleven provide you a lot of information on this subject.

Selling Cost

Advertising, marketing, city inspection fee, and the realtor's commission is included in this.

Closing Cost

Included in the closing cost are title charges, attorney fees, transfer taxes if charged in the specific city your property is located in, property taxes prorated, etc.

Once you total your estimate of all these numbers, subtract them from your expected sale price, and you are left with your profit. You determine how much makes it worthwhile for you. Determining what the sale price should be is discussed in Chapter Thirteen on marketing.

In the beginning it is important for you to be detailed about all this so it sticks in your mind well enough. Not until after you have the experience of completing several deals should you attempt estimating these numbers off the top of your head.

Preparing to Bid at the Foreclosure Auction

When preparing to bid, make sure you know if you are out bidding a first or second mortgage. A mistake here could be devastating. So now you want to know how to determine if it is a first mortgage. The most accurate method is to do a title search. This can be costly, as we know there are many more unsuccessful bids than successful bids. However, sometimes paying for a title search is necessary to make bidding be in your comfort zone. What I have done, and recommend that you do, is establish a relationship with the title company that you run most of your deals through. You can call your contact person, give them the address and tax number over the phone, and they search their computer to see the liens on the title. This does not give you a guarantee or warranty, but together with the other information you have gathered, it can make you comfortable.

Some methods for getting a good feeling of a mortgage position are:

- ♦ The older the date of the loan, the more likely it is a first mortgage. Although not conclusive, any loan beyond fifteen years is probably a

first. The oldest mortgage I have found in foreclosure was twenty nine years old.
- If you know that during a certain time period the first mortgage interest rates were around 9% and you see a rate of 14%, this may indicate to you it is probably a second mortgage. Second mortgages are typically at higher interest rates than first mortgages. However, there are also higher first mortgages with people who had credit problems when getting their mortgage.
- If the mortgage is an FHA or VA loan, it is a first mortgage. These governmental entities only insure first mortgages.
- You can call the attorney's office handling the foreclosure case. Ask them to verify for you if the mortgage is a first.

Do not become discouraged if most attorneys will not help you; that is typical. However, some will. Of course, this is no guarantee. In fact, none of the above methods are. They have worked well for me, and I have never gotten stung. The only guarantee available is paying for a policy of title insurance. You can do your own title search. It is called a track search. It involves researching the books in the county building, usually the recorders office, for the history on the subject property. It is all public information that is available to anyone willing to spend the time researching. Clerks are generally available to assist you. This process is time consuming.

Properties Not Bid On

On the properties in which the lender is the only bidder, which are FHA (Federal Housing Authority) insured, the properties are turned over to H.U.D (Housing of Urban Development). In some regions they first are offered to local non-profit organizations. Those remaining then appear on the H.U.D. list that is published in one of the major local newspapers and or on the internet. V.A. (Veterans Administration) insured properties appear on the V.A. list also in a major local newspaper and or on the internet.

The other properties become Bank Owned or more commonly known as R.E.O.'s (Real Estate Owned). They typically market them with a local real estate broker who specializes in R.E.O.'s. The big lenders who have R.E.O.'s all over the United States will not deal directly with individuals. They direct you to their real estate broker. Small local lenders will deal directly if you approach them prior to their assigning the property to a real estate broker.

CHAPTER 4

Approaching the Owner in Foreclosure

In the first stage of the foreclosure process owners are usually thinking in terms of keeping their home. However, their optimism can diminish as their debt increases with each passing day. Some people hang on right to the very end and lose all their equity. I have even had them tell me they are going to win the lottery. For most people they are on an emotional roller-coaster. One day they are thinking positive, going to find a way to get the money; the next day they are thinking, "Why keep trying, it is too hard, bad memories are here; anyway, if I sell, I can start fresh elsewhere." Of course, your objective is to contact them during one of their low periods. It is during these times that you have the best chance to get your foot in the door to establish some rapport.

Contacting the Owner

There are three ways to contact the owner:

- **Knock on their door**
- **Telephone**
- **Write a letter**

Of course, the most productive approach is personal contact.

Appearance

Dress nice but casual. Over-dressing will tend to put the owner more on guard. The same goes for driving up in an expensive car; this will not impress them. Be conservative. Yes, you are a business person, but you also need to be a person who cares. Listen intently as they tell you about their problems. You can learn much by listening, and this will help you in determining how to approach them in making a deal on their home.

The Introduction

The first time I knocked on a door a woman answered, I said; *"Hi! I know about your home being in foreclosure. Are you interested in selling?"* Slam! Went the door. Needless to say I refined my approach.

When the home owner answers the door or the phone, ask for Mr. or Mrs. _____ and introduce yourself. I usually say something like, *"Hi. My name is Allen Watkins. I work with people having difficulties with their mortgage. I may be able to help you with your circumstances. May I talk with you for a few minutes?"* Any basic approach like this is non-threatening and is not offensive. You have to remember these people are on an emotional roller-coaster. Anyone would be sensitive having a stranger approach them about their financial problems.

Sometimes they will allow you to set an appointment or invite you in. However, the majority of the time they will tell you, "It is already taken care of." Whether it is or not, they tell you this to get rid of you. The response to this is: *"Great, I wish you the best of luck! May I ask how you have taken care of it?"* Some typical responses are: *"My attorney is taking care of it. We are going to pay it off. We are refinancing. We have it sold."* Then say, *"Good, hope it works out! May I leave you my name and number in case it falls through?"* Do not be offended or take it personally if they should slam the door in your face. You just caught them at a bad time. I do not advise for you to knock on the door again. You could leave a note on the door with your name and number. Plan to keep track of the case and prepare for the auction if you feel its worthwhile. See Case In Point # 4, Burbank.

Whether or not you get in, you are observing. In fact, you take note of the curb appeal, condition of the exterior, siding, windows, fascia, soffit, gutters, and roof. I think you get the picture. Also, while you are standing at the front door and it is open, take note of what you can see on the interior.

What if there is no answer? Then what? Leave a note, similar to the letter you would mail. If you question whether or not someone even lives in the property, inquire with the neighbors. They can sometimes provide much insight into the property and the people who lived, there.

When Vacant

If the home appears vacant, but you are not sure, walk around to the back and check the electric meter. If it is not moving, the electricity is off, and most likely the home is vacant. You should try to confirm this with a neighbor. For my first one, see case in point # 7, Streamwood.

You may be wondering why people would leave or abandon their property. I am sure there are many reasons, but I will tell you some of the reasons I have encountered.

- **Death:** There are no relatives, or the relatives do not care or do not have the ability to take care of the property — especially when the property is over indebted, and sometimes even when there is considerable equity. See Case in Point # 18, DesPlaines.
- **Running from the law or in jail:** I have had several instances of this. One I heard about from a neighbor. The husband abused his wife. One night she had enough and shot him to death. Now she was in jail.
- **Fear:** Some people do not know the foreclosure process. The summons scared them, and they felt they had to get out right away before the sheriff put them out.
- **Transfer:** Some need to move for job, medical, or family reasons.
- **Bad memories:** Some people become tired and emotionally drained from all the personal problems. Instead of attacking their problems, they run from them. They are anxious for a new start in life.

When you have established that the house is vacant, what next?

Locating the Owner

- Talk to the neighbors. Tell the neighbors you are an investor and want to buy the property. If you buy it, you will be cleaning it up and putting money into it which will improve the neighborhood and their property.
- Leave a handwritten note on the mail box (legally you are not supposed to put anything inside the mail box), inside the screen or storm door, or in the window. Sometimes the owner is coming back at night to pick up the mail, or a neighbor picks it up for them.
- Mail two letters. The first one with a letter, and the second one with a letter, also however, on this one under your return address print "ADDRESS RETURN REQUESTED." If they left a forwarding address you will now get it.
- Call information to get their phone number. Sometimes when people move they have the phone company give out their new number via a recording. If there is no phone number for the listed address, call other names in the phone book, especially if the name is an unusual one, because you can most likely locate a relative. Case in Point # 5, Barry.

- Go to the county building where the foreclosure file is. Use the case number to request the file. In it will be a copy of the sheriff's summons. It will show where the sheriff served the owner, or if the sheriff was able to locate them.
- Call the utility companies to see where the water, gas, or electric bill is sent.

Granted the utility companies may not give just anybody the information. Therefore, pose as the owner and say, *"I have not received my last billing statement. Would you tell me what address you are mailing it to?"*

- Call the county tax assessor to see where the tax bill is being sent.
- Call the local veterinarian. People with pets contact their veterinarian when they move.

When asking people for information to help you locate the owner you may want to mention that the person your looking for may have some money coming from the last house they lived in. That is why your trying to locate them.

- If the ownership is in a land trust, write a letter to the bank. On the envelope state "Attention land trust department, trust # _____." The bank must forward the letter to the owner unopened.
- Call the foreclosing attorney. Occasionally the owner has been in contact with them and may have given a phone number. I have had an attorney pass an owner's phone number on to me.

These are some of the activities that skip tracers perform to locate people. If you are unsuccessful in locating the owner or if they are uncooperative once you locate them, simply follow the property through the foreclosure process and show up at the auction.

Writing Letters

Writing letters is perhaps the least effective method however, it is still productive when you do not have the time to knock on the door or call. I recommend not using your home address. Use a P.O. Box if you have no other options. The company Mail Boxes Etc. offers P.O. boxes and gives you a regular address with a suite number for the box number. Be sure to use first class postage to insure your letters will be forwarded or returned.

Here are some sample letters that can serve as a guide for you:

1. This letter is money for you. Solve your foreclosure problem. I can save your credit and give you some money for your equity. I will pay all your

The Reality of Real Estate Investing

back payments, late charges, court costs, and attorney fees, thus saving your credit.

The longer you wait to contact me the sooner the lender will be able to foreclose. As time goes on, I will be able to pay you less money for your equity.

Call now to save your credit and receive maximum dollars for your equity.

2. I would like to offer you help regarding your property. I can give you cash for your equity and save your credit. I have helped other people save their credit. A foreclosure affects your credit for many years. At the very least, I can answer some questions for you about the foreclosure process.
3. You will soon lose your property at a foreclosure sale. You must do something now. I will give you cash for your equity, save your credit, and help you get a new, fresh start.
4. I will give you cash to solve your problems and allow you to continue living in your house. You can continue to enjoy your home without loss of credit or reputation.
5. I work with people having problems with their mortgage. I can help in one of the following ways:

   A. Refinance and pay off your existing mortgage, or provide financing to just bring you current.
   B. Sell quickly for cash so that you can maximize your efforts for a fresh start.

Call me today! If nothing else, perhaps I can just answer some questions about the foreclosure process.

If you are a licensed realtor, legally you must disclose this fact. Having been on both sides of the street, I consider this a benefit. You are viewed as a professional. You can state that you specialize in working with or helping people in foreclosure. I have listed and sold many homes prior to the owner losing their home from my letter. Sometimes this has involved discounting the first, second or third lien holder to allow a sale to happen. Then this has gotten my foot in the door to establish a new R.E.O. client.

Questions to Ask

Now you are in the home with the owner. What do you say or do? The first thing to remember is, as I mentioned earlier, listen to what the owner has to say. Basically you play it by ear how to respond or what to ask, depending on what the owner is saying. You learn and fine tune your approach with practice and experience.

Always use the words property or house instead of home. You want to distance them from the emotional ties as much as possible. The answer to this first question helps you determine the direction of your conversation.

Some suggestions would be:

- Are you thinking in terms of keeping the property or selling and getting a fresh new start?
- Would you mind if we started with a tour of the property so I can see what the layout of the house is and the repairs that are needed?
- What repairs are you aware of?
- What caused the mortgage to get behind?
- How much do you owe on your first mortgage? What are the monthly payments? How many months behind are you?
- Is it a conventional, FHA, or VA mortgage?
- Do you have any other liens against the property?
- Are you behind with them?
- Have you tried to do anything yet to solve your problem? If so, what?
- What do you feel the value is?
- What makes you feel the value is _____?
- Realistically, what would you like to happen?
- Are you the only owner? Or is someone else on the title with you?

Obviously you are asking probing questions mixed up with some factual questions to give you a better overall picture of their scenario and a feeling about where they are coming from. Of course, you do not just rapid fire all these questions at them; ask them throughout your conversation with them, as you gain rapport. Be complimentary - cute kids, good mannered dog, etc. Steer clear of mentioning positive things about the house. You are pointing out and making notes on the negatives in a subtle manner. Only with practice and experience will you fine tune your abilities here.

Making a deal with owners does not necessarily mean buying their property at a cheap price. Although it happens, it is rare that an owner will simply turn over thousands of dollars of equity to you. It all depends on the owner's mind set. See Case in Point # 5, Barry and # 20, Wentworth.

Sometimes you can help an owner keep his property and earn a fee for your service. This is discussed further in Chapter Five.

When you are first starting out of course you feel like you know nothing, and you want to know more. You want to be able to approach and respond to the owner perfectly. Well, you just have to accept the fact that you cannot and will not know enough until you are actually doing it. You will make mistakes; when you do, you will learn from them. Accept this as a part of the process. Keep in mind, you at least have this book to establish a foundation. The owners know very little or nothing.

There is nothing wrong with admitting that you are new at this or that you do not know the answer to a question. Most of the time this will put them in the frame of mind of trying to help you. Remember the murder mystery show "Colombo" the murderers were trying to help him solve the case because he played as if he did not know much. Assure the owner that you are working with a partner who will help you, or that you will find out the answer to their question. Then be sure to follow up.

CHAPTER 5

Making Deals / Money with the Owner

The first point I would like to emphasize is that sometimes you find yourself answering questions, giving advice, and not making money. I advocate providing a service to help people in foreclosure. If that means helping them and not earning a dime or selling quickly for cash and your earning a handsome profit, great! The reward of knowing you just helped a fellow human being is very satisfying. Obviously, you can not afford to do just this unless perhaps you are a philanthropist. The fact of the matter is, as long as you are out there making contacts and have a creative mind set, you will find plenty of opportunities for making money. Lots of money!

When a deal is made, the owner should be satisfied; his burden lifted. Now he can get a fresh start in life. However, if this involves coercion, deceit, manipulating, or anything you would not be comfortable telling your mom, children, great-grandchildren, or God about, do not do it! I believe in the Golden Rule, and what goes around comes around. We are not put on this earth to see through one another; we are put here to see one another through!

After asking your probing questions, building rapport, and listening, you will have a feeling of what the owner is thinking. What are they most interested in doing? It boils down to either keeping or getting rid of the house.

Profit Centers

In dealing directly with the owner, some strategies to make money are:

- ► **Management Technique**
- ► **Purchase**
- ► **Selling**
- ► **Sale / Lease Back with Option Technique**
- ► **Referral**

Management Technique

When I first started in this business, I was really excited about making deals with people. I started by mailing out letters because I was part of a company publishing information on all the foreclosure filings in the five county area around Chicago. This gave me the information on literally hundreds of foreclosures every week. I did not want a single lead to slip through my fingers. Mailing letters was the only way to cover them all. When some of the letters started coming back stamped by the post office "Moved / Left No Address" or "Vacant," I was excited! I figured I knew there was a reason for motivation because of the foreclosure. Now perhaps there was a double reason for motivation because of the home also being vacant. Focusing on these leads alone kept me busy.

When I found a house vacant, I felt there was no reason I should not be able to create a positive circumstance out of this negative situation. I soon learned that vacant homes are usually a sign that they are over-indebted. People do not usually just walk away from equity — unless it is a death situation, job transfer, etc. Sometimes in a divorce the woman is left with the house, knowing it is over-indebted. She is not familiar with how long the foreclosure process is and will go ahead and move out. See Case in Point # 7, Streamwood.

At this point you have to decide what direction to take. Your options are:

- **Pass it up as not being worthwhile.**
- **Attempt to locate the owner.**
- **Keep an eye on it until it goes to auction.**
- **Buy from the lender once they own it.**
- **Rent during the foreclosure process.**

My philosophy is to act quickly and go in the direction of making the quickest possible deal. Certainly while in the stages of foreclosure, the owner is the source.

If there is reasonable equity, I will work on negotiating a deal with the owner. If there is not enough equity, then I will also contact the lender about discounting to make it worthwhile. If that does not work out, then the situation is that the house is vacant and will just sit there deteriorating until it goes to auction and then back to the lender. That is when I approach the owner about renting the house out.

I have rented homes from as little as three months to eighteen months during the foreclosure process. See Case in Point # 11, Summit. This is a positive situation for all involved. You and the owner make money. Once the lender gets ownership, he receives the home in better condition than it otherwise would have been had it remained vacant all those months. Plus, the tenant is a potential purchaser from you if you are able to make a deal with the bank once they own it. You can then simply sell immediately to your tenant at a higher price. Also, you have the opportunity during the foreclosure process (lease period) to help the tenants get pre-approved for financing, correct any credit issues, or help them build up a down payment. This could come in part as a credit from part of the rent they have paid you. Or, you could arrange for the tenant to buy directly from the bank and earn a commission if you are licensed. This is not possible with FHA or VA insured loans. These governmental agencies require that the homes become vacant before they are placed on their marketing list.

If I felt I could clean up, paint, and take care of necessary repairs for an amount less than the first and last month's rent, then I would feel it would be feasible to rent the house. I would collect that much up front from the tenant anyway. Sometimes I have had to do nothing or very little, or I would structure a deal with the tenant to do the work.

Once I have determined that the situation is qualified as a "rent until the bank takes it back" scenario, then I discuss the benefits with the owner as mentioned above and that it reduces their liability, in the following ways:

- Some repairs are done, and the home is maintained in a liveable condition, giving it more value for the bank when the bank sells the property. When the proceeds are not enough to cover the debt, the bank can go after the ex-owner for a deficiency judgment for the monies still due. It actually becomes a personal judgment against them.
- You will start paying the homeowner's insurance that they have stopped paying, thereby reducing their risk if the house should burn down or someone is hurt while walking across the yard.
- Their conscience will feel better knowing that they have chosen the most responsible action available to them.
- They will feel better knowing their property will not be the eyesore of the neighborhood. Their neighbors will not be thinking badly of them.
- There is no cost to them for expenses and your time. You will be compensated from the rent collected.
- Finally, and best of all, they do not have to do anything but give you permission by signing a simple management agreement.

The following is a sample that can be pre-typed on your letterhead.

Owner: _____ Manager: _____
It is hereby agreed on this date _____, that the owner of the house located at _____, gives permission to _____ to manage and lease out said address.

The compensation for management will be derived solely from the rents collected.

It is further agreed that the owner will be paid ____% of the net rents collected after all expenses are paid first.

A basic simple agreement like this is all I have ever used.

If some concern came up for the owner and I was agreeable to it I would just write it on the agreement.

There is one more benefit that I sometimes offer the owner; however, it depends on the over-all situation. You are the one who is sticking your neck out financially for the initial repairs, insurance, utilities, advertising, and your time. In a tight situation I might offer the owner nothing more than the benefits just mentioned. In better situations I would agree to pay the owner 25% - 50% of the net rental income. This means the rent money left over after paying all the expenses.

You may be wondering what I tell the tenants about the circumstances with the house their renting. That is a fair question, I would explain the situation as it is, and then put this clause in the lease:

Lessee is aware that this home is in the process of foreclosure. Once completed the lender may become the new landlord or may retain our management service. Should lessee be interested in purchasing the home, every effort will be made in helping them accomplish that goal.

I would only give them a month-to-month lease because I could not guarantee a year due to the legal process. However, as an incentive to rent the home, I would give a discounted rent of $100 - $200 off the market rent for the area. This program has worked very well! See Case in Point # 11, Summit. My first two months working this program produced $11,000 in profit. Of course, that was all I focused on. As time went on and I started purchasing properties, I focused less and less on management deals.

Purchase

If you determine from your conversation that the owner wants to sell, your next question should be: *"How much do you need to move?"* Note that I used the word "need," not want or would like to have. Sometimes all that is needed is just enough money to pay moving expenses or first month's rent and security deposit. Even though a property may have equity to you, to the owner all it may have is bad memories.

When the owner is in the frame of mind to make a deal, you do not delay. See Case in Point # 5, Barry and # 25, Crete. Time is of the essence! You do not necessarily give the owner money at this point. The rule that applies is that you do not give them any significant amount of money until they give you the keys and possession. However, you do put your agreement in writing. Give them as little as you can get away with; $10 to $25 to seal the deal, and the balance due and payable upon closing. A general sales contract from your local office supply will do. However, do not delay putting your agreement in writing while waiting for proper forms. I have even heard of investors putting an agreement on a napkin. As long as it is in writing, it is legal. It is not as if you would actually sue an owner for specific performance should they fail to perform according to the agreement. It would not be worth it in most cases. However, it does commit the owner more firmly, to have it in writing with his signature. Also, refer to Chapter 12, Contracts and Clauses. If the situation is right, you fill out a Warranty Deed or Quick Claim Deed immediately and get the other spouse or whomever else is on the title to a notary.

Selling

Should you determine there is just not enough equity or profit margin for you to purchase the property, and you know you are not able to discount the lien holder to create that profit margin, or the owner and bank is negotiable but just not enough, the next possibility is to sell the property for the owner to a home buyer and earn a fee for doing so. You might be thinking, *"Why wouldn't the owner just sell it themselves and avoid a fee to me?"* Remember that emotionally the owner just may not be able to put forth that effort and deal with it; therefore, you help them. See Case in Point # 12, Evergreen Park.

If you have a license, sell the home and earn a commission as you normally would. If you do not, you cannot legally earn a commission without a license. You could refer the situation to a Realtor to sell and earn the commission. However, again you cannot earn a referral fee without a license. You could work out a deal with the Realtor to discount the commission rate to you when they sell a home for you in the future. Or, you could actually sign a contract to purchase the property from the owner for a set price. Sign the contract with your name and / or assignee. Then find a buyer for a higher price and basically assign your contract to the buyer you have found. You will need to consult with your attorney to work out the details of accomplishing what is referred to as the "double closing." This is legal because you actually have something tangible to sell, which is your contract and your right to buy the property.

Sale / Lease Back with Option

This simply means the owner sells to you and you then enter into a lease agreement and an option agreement for the owner to rent and then buy the house back after a given point in time. This works well when the owners want to keep their home and they have considerable equity. This also works well when the problem that caused them to get behind in the first place has been resolved.

I will share with you a structure of one of these deals.

First and foremost, however you structure it, there must be a reasonable possibility of the owners being able to keep to the deal and exercise their option.

The Reality of Real Estate Investing

Keep in mind should the owners fail to exercise their option, all the equity is yours. If that owner then hires an attorney who determines you were unscrupulous and structured the deal with the intention of the owner failing, guess what? You lose! In fact, once you have an agreed deal with the owner, include on the contract your recommendation that they have an attorney review it for them. The best case scenario is that they do it, and you document it.

Example:

    Home valued at ———— $120,000
    Balance owed ———— $ 57,000
    Repairs needed ———— $ 5,000
    ———Equity ———————— $ 58,000

This example involves no cash out of pocket, only use of your credit. The owner deeds the property over to you. You then refinance the property to pay off the existing balance owed or take out an equity loan to bring their loan current. The amount of the loan should be enough to cover the following expenses:

- All liens paid off or brought current.
- Taxes brought current.
- Homeowner's insurance for one year.
- Their attorney fee and yours.
- All associated closing costs.
- Three to six months rent payments up front.
- Three year's worth of premiums for term life insurance naming you as the beneficiary for the amount of the loan.
- Three year's worth of premiums for disability insurance to protect monthly rental payments in the event the bread winner of the family becomes disabled.
- Money to take care of any needed repairs.
- Five to ten thousand dollars of profit for you. This can be termed as the option fee.

Three years should be long enough for the owners to get their act together and accomplish exercising their option to purchase. If they are able to exercise the option at the end of the first year, great; they pay the balance owed. From one year and one day to two years, the purchase price increases by $1,000. From two years and one day to three years, it is $2,000 more. After three years they lose all rights. The equity is all yours. However, in order to ensure the ex-tenant with option to buy cooperates with you to sell the property, you could agree that they would still receive a certain percentage of the net proceeds at the closing and upon their turning over the keys and possession to the new buyer.

Rent payments should be about $25 more than your monthly principal, interest, taxes, and insurance. You personally contract and supervise any work to be done to the property.

In the beginning as you are explaining the deal to the owners, let them know you are structuring it so strictly because this is a second chance for them and you want them to succeed with the agreement. Should the bread winner become deceased or disabled, the other spouse will be cleared of having to worry about making the house payments because of the life and disability insurance. Be sure to also explain the downside clearly. That is, they will lose the house and the remaining equity should they fall behind again. Make it clear, put it in writing, and have them sign it. The main idea of your doing a lease option, of course, is that in the event of a default, all you have to do is a tenant eviction versus making them a loan and then having to foreclose.

Referral

Perhaps you are unable or unwilling to use the method above. Instead of just walking away from the deal, you could refer it to someone who would be willing to do it. Then work out a finder's fee.

What if the owner wants to sell and the amount he wants or debt versus value is too much for you to profit? It is still not a lost cause; you have a couple of options.

A. Refer the seller to a real estate broker and work out compensation. Of course, this could be incentive for you to get your own real estate license. Also, consider the commissions you could save on your own residence and investments. A realtor can only legally pay a referral fee to another licensed realtor. Therefore, when I say compensation, you need to be creative. For example, you can barter reduced commissions when the agent sells property for you, or you can utilize the realtor's services in helping you determine the value of properties you are pursuing.

B. First enter into a contract to purchase with the owner's agreeable price and one little clause — *subject to purchaser being able to discount the pay off balance of the lien holders, to his satisfaction.* Any discounts will result in a reduced purchase price by the discounted amount. The seller's net proceeds at closing remain the same. You sign the deal and then negotiate with the lien holders to earn your profit. If you are unsuccessful, you are not obligated.

As you get involved I am sure your own creative brain waves will come up with even more ideas.

The Law of Possibility

Nothing is impossibile to the person who knows who they are and what they want, and is willing to put forth the effort towards the attainment of everything they want, and wish to become.

CHAPTER 6

Approaching the Lender

There are different types of lenders:

- **Banks**
- **Mortgage companies**
- **Finance companies**

To deal directly with them, you will find that smaller companies are easier to work with. Many of the larger lenders have exclusive contracts with real estate brokers, and they will refer you directly to them. I know this first hand because I am one of these brokers. However, this is not a negative! This is especially true for the beginner who may be uncomfortable dealing direct. Also, a good broker will be very helpful in the decision making and deal-making process.

Now I know you are thinking, *"The broker probably buys up all the good deals!"* This is simply not the case. First of all, to be successful in selling R.E.O.'s (Real Estate Owned properties), it has to be the main focus for the real estate broker. When done right, brokerage is also lucrative. I am sure other brokers, as I do, occasionally buy some property on their own behalf. However, no one person or group of people can buy them all. There are just too many. There are literally thousands in different stages of the process all the time. As my mentor responded to my comment when I was first starting out and said, *"Gee, Gary, there sure seems to be a lot of competition,"* *"Yes Allen, it was no different when I started* twenty *years ago; there is always room for one more. As long as you are consistently and persistently chasing them, you will make deals."* I have proven his statement to be true, and probably for every new person getting into the business, another one is retiring.

Some bigger lenders turn all their R.E.O.'S over to management referral companies, who then refer them to real estate brokers. Small lenders will be happy to talk with you directly. Some will even meet with you to show you the property; of course, you have established in their minds that you are a serious buyer. They especially enjoy the sound of the words, *"I am a cash buyer and can close as soon as you can!"*

Locating the lender and then the right person to talk to is not always an easy task. However, persistence does pay off.

Contact Sources

- **Yellow Pages**
- **Home Owner or Foreclosure Legal Notices**
- **Attorneys**
- **Lender Directories**
- **Walk Right into the Bank**

Yellow Pages

The yellow pages can be an excellent starting point. Many of my successful lender relationships began with the yellow pages. You call a bank up, and when a receptionist or clerk answers, you ask, *"Does your company have an R.E.O. department?"* The clerk says, *"Yes. Should I transfer you?"* You say, *"No. Would you give me their direct phone number?"* Then have the clerk transfer you. The clerk may tell you their R.E.O. department is located at their headquarters or regional office, and give you the number. If it is long-distance, ask the clerk if they have an 800 number. Of course, that is a question you would only ask a clerk, not the R.E.O. manager.

The clerk may not know what R.E.O. means. Tell her, *"Real Estate Owned, properties your bank has foreclosed on and now owns."* Ask to speak with the person responsible for properties they foreclose on. This may help the clerk help you, and if not, ask to speak to their manager and start again.

Once you are talking to the person responsible for their R.E.O.'s, simply tell them you are a cash investor — only if you actually are, of course. You can be even if you do not have the money yourself. I discuss this further in Chapter Eight "Creative Financing." Ask if they have any properties to sell right now? If they do, ask for the basic information - address, description, and price. You can then decide if you want to do a drive-by first or go ahead and set an appointment to see the inside. If they have several, then they may have a list they could mail or fax to you.

Keep in mind that not all lenders are anxious to admit they have foreclosures. They do not know if you are really an investor or one of their major depositors checking on them. Some lenders are embarrassed about their R.E.O.'s which represent mistakes, bad loans, and quite often loss of money. Also, bear in mind if you already have an address that this lender is foreclosing on or has foreclosed on (such as from a legal notice or from a home owner), you will sometimes get further with the R.E.O. manager.

Once done with the information about that specific address, you ask, *"Do you have any other properties I might be interested in?"*

Home Owners / Foreclosure Legal Notice

When you are dealing with the owner in foreclosure, get the lender's name and number. You will need to have the owner call first, to give the lender permission to talk with you. Now you can talk with the lender about the details of the loan. You may just need a payoff letter. Ask the lender to include in the payoff letter an itemization of the monies owed — principal balance, interest due, late fees, attorney fees, or any other fees included in the payoff. On occasion I have found fees that were not reasonable. Upon questioning them, I got those fees removed. Keep in mind that a lender has to get all fees approved by a judge while going through the foreclosure process. That is not the case when the loan is being brought current or paid off.

Calling the Attorney

Call the attorney handling the foreclosure case. Some attorneys are helpful; some are not. My opinion about attorneys handling foreclosure cases is this: The lender is their client. They should do what is in the best interest of their client. The lender's objective is to get this non-performing loan paid off as soon as possible. It stands to reason that anything the attorney can do to facilitate this should be done. Among other things this includes assisting investors with needed information (that is public information anyway) to make a decision about pursuing a property. Some understand this and are easy to work with; others will not give investors the time of day. I believe if the lender / client knew that potential cash buyers were being blown off by their attorney, he would not be representing them any more.

It is best when calling the attorneys to see if you can get your questions answered by their secretary or paralegal. They will sometimes be more helpful. When calling, you can say, *"I'm calling on the foreclosure case* (or *foreclosure auction case*) *of XYZ lender vs. John and Mary Smith."* Be prepared with the foreclosure case number and the attorney's file number if available. These numbers will appear on the legal notice and on the complaint of foreclosure in the court file. When the owner is served the summons by the sheriff, the complaint of foreclosure also comes attached.

Some questions you may ask:

- Is XYZ Bank's mortgage a first or second mortgage?
- I see from the legal notice or court file that the judgment amount is _____. Do you have a more up-dated figure?
- Are there any other liens? If the answer is yes, ask if their has been any response from the other lien holders who are intending to represent their interest at the auction?

The Reality of Real Estate Investing

- If it is true, you might say, *"Looks like the debt is more than the value for a cash buyer. Do you think the lender might open the bidding with less than what they are owed? You know, I might even be interested in buying the loan from the lender?"* Listen for their response.
- Can you put me in touch with XYZ lender?

If the answer is no, ask if they will tell you the town and state where the lender is located or provide you with other useful information. See Case in Point # 10, West Chicago.

These are probing questions. Which ones you ask will depend on the circumstances you are dealing with. The more you actually attempt to do this the more effective you will become.

Always speak with a friendly attitude. You never know when you might come across this same attorney in the future on another deal. For every contact you make, put the name and number in your phone directory or rolodex with a note or two of information to help you remember your last contact with that person.

Lender Directories

You can check at your local library for a directory of lenders across the country; banks, mortgage companies, finance companies, etc. Also check the internet.

Walk Right into a Bank

First impressions are important. Be sure to dress business-like not too casual. The first thing you want to do is acquire a copy of the bank's **Statement of Condition**. Usually it is in the form of a simple brochure. This is a financial statement of the bank's assets and liabilities. Sometimes this is located in plain view on the counter. Other times you may have to ask for it at the information counter. Under the assets column you will find words that state something like **Real Estate Owned & / or in judgment 853.** The number on the right side represents thousands of dollars, the above would be $853,000.00. Now armed with this information, you basically follow the same verbiage as with the phone approach. Only now if you are told they do not have any foreclosure properties, you pull out their Statement of Condition, open it up, and say, *"Are you sure you are not mistaken? According to your Statement of Condition, you currently have $853,000.00 worth of foreclosures."* The bank representative will usually double check and then talk with you about their properties.

As a final thought for this chapter, if you think you need to wait until you know or remember it all, then you are never going to do it. Some of your most valuable learning takes place while you are doing it. Just get to it and do it! Resign yourself to the fact that you are going to make some mistakes. That is all right because you will be learning and getting closer to your first deal and money in your pocket.

There is a fine line difference on perspective between getting involved and being committed.

In ham and eggs, the chicken is involved, but the pig is committed.

John Allen Price

CHAPTER 7

Making Deals / Money with Lenders

The very best strategy in making a deal with any lender is from a position of "CASH!" My experience has always been that a lender would rather sell quickly, at a lower price than at a higher price over time or subject to financing.

There are exceptions. Some finance companies would like an opportunity to place a new loan on the property. A new face, good credit, and financial strength is what they are in business for. Points and interest rates are typically higher than what one could get from their own bank. However, for some this is a good alternative when the opportunity exists.

Purchasing / Discounting the Mortgage

When dealing with lenders prior to their getting ownership of a property, you may be talking to them about a pay-off to complete a sale with the owner. You also may talk to them when the owner cannot be found or is uncooperative. Then you may consider buying the mortgage note if the circumstances warrant it. Sometimes you will willingly pay full value for the mortgage note. This means the total amount owed. Other times you will work on discounting or paying as far below the amount owed as you can. See Case in Point # 1, Harlem Ave ; # 5, Barry ; and # 9 Foster Ave.

There are some inherent **advantages** and **risk** to doing this. One advantage is that you are now the person in control, and you call the shots. Of course, in order to get the deed and profit, you must complete the foreclosure process unless you simply turn around and sell the note to another investor for more than you paid. However, in most cases you will be interested in a bigger piece of the pie.

Your conversation should start something like this:

"Hi, Mr. / Ms _____. My name is _____. I am an investor, and I am trying to work out a deal on one of your non- performing loans. The loan number is _____."

Then you ask for the amount due. Sometimes you will get all the information you need right then, or you may just get a ball park figure, or they will prepare a payoff letter for you. Whatever the case, before the conversation is done you are going to slip in a comment like, *"If I am able to help Mr._____ payoff this loan in the very near future, would you consider discounting the balance due to get it off your books?"* Be quiet and wait for a response. Always be sure to use the word "**if**" in the beginning of a statement like this because you are not committing yourself to paying it off — only "**if**" you did. You are not asking for the lender to discount a specific number; just in general terms would a discount be considered. You are trying to get a feel for what you might or might not be able to do. However the lender responds, say you will see what you can put together and will get back to him.

Also, when you are dealing with large multi-units or commercial real estate, price and terms can become more flexible. See Case in Point # 13, 76 unit. My mentor has made the following comment: "*If someone owes the bank $5,000 and can not pay it back, they have a problem. If someone owes the bank $5,000,000 and can not pay it back, the bank has a problem*!"

Making deals / money with lenders can be the same as with any seller. It is a matter of making offers that make good business sense for you. It is a numbers' game; the more offers you make, the better your chance of getting one accepted.

Typically your biggest profit margins will be in properties that need work. Occasionally you can find a property in a nice, move-in condition far enough below value to make it worthwhile. However, you will need to close quickly with cash. Most lenders are not fools. Notice I said, "most." I have seen some do surprising things. See Case in Point #14, Natchez. If they have a home in move-in condition worth $150,000, they know it can sell quickly to a home buyer at $140,000. However, if they only have $90,000 in it, and the lender is in a desperate situation, he will sometimes sell quickly to an investor. For example, a lender's fiscal year is about to end, and he gets a bonus based on how good his books look, or a penalty based on how bad his books look. If he has a high number of non-performing loans, judgments pending, and real estate owned, of course he would be tempted to accept an offer that makes him look better prior to his deadline.

I have one lender client that I have sold a couple hundred properties for over the last couple of years. He gets bonuses monthly based on how many he sells and closes. He is always more flexible on offers that close quickly by the end of the month.

Another method to increase your profit margin in dealing with lenders is to buy in bulk. Make a package offer to buy several of their properties. That gives them incentive to give you a better price.

Buying Before the Auction

You can acquire an interest in a property prior to its going to the foreclosure auction by doing one of the following:

1. Making a deal with the owner and having him sign over all his rights and interest via a Quick Claim Deed. See Case in Point # 25 Crete.
2. Making a deal with the lender and having him sign over all the banks rights and interest in the mortgage note. You now step into the shoes of the lender. It is a very common practice for mortgage companies to sell their paper to other mortgage companies. In this case they would just sell to you, an investor.

Now you continue the foreclosure process to get the deed. See Case in Point # 15, Dickens. Now that you own the position of the lender, you have control over the auction. When it goes to auction, it is possible you will be over-bid. That could be OK if you paid less than the balance owed on the note, but maybe you paid the full amount owed on the note, or again you want a bigger piece of the pie. Therefore, you bid in at the auction and hope for the best. In the worst case you will get all your money back. If another investor bids after the opening bid, you do have the option of bidding yourself. However, know that the amount of money between your opening bid and the successful bid goes first to junior lien holders and then to the ex-homeowner. This is not automatic. A motion has to be filed and an order entered by a judge before any money is released. It goes to the state after seven years if it is never claimed.

Buying at the Auction

The very best method for buying from lenders is to simply out-bid them at the foreclosure auction. There you do not need them to say yes; you just bid a dollar more than their opening bid, and it is yours — unless there are other bidders. Then it is the successful bidder.

After doing your homework, the next step is making sure you show up on time. See Case in Point # 8, Rockwell. Make sure you are prepared with sufficient deposit money. I have been challenged, and I have seen savvy investors challenge other bidders on having all their deposit money. Some auctioneers have learned to require bidders to show their deposit prior to their bid.

Buying after the Auction

You probably thought once the auction took place and a successful bid was entered, that was it. There is always opportunity awaiting the creative mind.

You could still make a deal with the owner and present it to the lender or their attorney prior to the motion before a Judge to approve the sale. If that does not work then hire an attorney to appear at the motion before the Judge and plead the case. Then the Judge will decide if your deal should be allowed to go through.

If the homeowner is uncooperative, or you are unable to locate the owner, there is still the lender. Although there is no longer a mortgage to buy, there is the Certificate of Sale. Simply put, you are again buying and stepping into the position of the lender. You wait out the redemption period and then get the deed. See Case in Point # 1, Harlem Ave.

If another investor was the successful bidder, you could also approach him to purchase his position.

Where there is no redemption period after the sale, a Certificate of Sale is still issued. The attorneys for the lender schedule a motion on the presiding judge's calendar to request an order approving the sale. You can still negotiate to buy the certificate from the lender during this time period. Or, you can even buy from the ex-owner as discussed in Chapter Six. I have seen deals made with the owner after the auction and prior to the judge's approval of sale. If the lender will not cooperate at this point (once a deal is struck), then an attorney for the owner can appear at the motion for approval. Request the judge to allow the deal to go through even though the lender's attorney may be opposing it. You see, legally it is all over. The owner has no rights and technically is now the ex-owner. However, the decision is on the shoulders of the judge. If he sees that the lender can be made whole, and the poor homeowner who is losing his home can still get something, he may judge in his favor.

Earlier I mentioned **advantages** and **risk**. I did not forget about the **risk**. When you buy out the lender's mortgage, you also assume their risk. Should the owner file bankruptcy any time up to the minute of the auction, the process is postponed and you have to wait two, three, or more months. The case goes before a Bankruptcy Judge. He could allow the owner a reorganization of his debts, and you could be stuck with your money tied up and just getting monthly payments. The judge could also dismiss the bankruptcy or dismiss the property from the bankruptcy. This process could take several months, a year, or more.

I have performed the possibilities described herein. My advice is to never buy a mortgage unless you are very confident the owner will not be filing bankruptcy. See Case in Point # 9, Foster.

Working with Realtors

Working with Realtors is profitable also, especially since some lenders only market through Realtors. Try to find agents / brokers who specialize in marketing R.E.O.'s. Search through the ads, newspapers, home magazines, etc. Look for agents advertising Foreclosures or Bank Owned Properties. Consider offering them a buyer's commission for locating a profitable deal. You want to establish a reputation of being a serious investor, ready to pay cash, and closing quickly. Realtors sometimes know about a property two to four weeks before it is actually put on the market through the M.L.S. Lenders will contact them to do drive-by inspections to check on occupancy and negotiate for possession. When vacant, they are responsible for getting locks changed, winterizing it, etc. Then the lender will usually order an appraisal, compare it with the Realtor's opinion of value, and decide on a list price. That is when the property is entered into the M.L.S. and is officially on the market.

If you have ever looked at an M.L.S. computer print-out on a property and noticed the marketing time was only one day, this is because the listing realtor told the buyer about it ahead of time.

Note: Once Realtors are given the official authorization to place a property on the market, they are required to get it in the M.L.S. computer system within twenty-four hours. That is the rule, however, it is not easy to monitor and enforce. For the most part I believe most Realtors comply.

CHAPTER 8

Creative Financing

One does not need to have a healthy bank account to be able to buy properties. Sure, it is helpful. However, I can tell you from personal experience that you can be a pauper and succeed in real estate.

A Little Personal History

I had meager beginnings. My family way back on both sides are people of strong fiber and character, hardworking, but poor. My parents continued in that tradition. Oh, we were not destitute or anything like that. We always had food on the table and a roof over our heads. (I was the oldest of four boys.) I remember one Christmas when money was tight, and all Dad and Mom were able to afford was a pair of gloves for each of us and a camera to share. Do not get me wrong; we had more good Christmases than not, and I am not complaining. I am thankful because I know there are those who had it much worse. My point in sharing this with you is to say, "*If I can do it, so can you!*"

As a teenager I learned to work hard. I made a commitment to myself that I was going to find a way to achieve financial independence. I could have graduated from high school, but I did not. Lacking maturity and wisdom, (during this time of my life) I instead dropped out and joined the U.S. Navy. I spent five years there, got my G.E.D., and worked in the medical field. During my last two years I worked nights in the emergency room at a Naval Medical Center and went to college during the day. I had gotten married and had my first son. There seemed to never be enough money. I went to school days, worked nights and part time on weekends delivering pizza, and still could not make ends meet.

I felt strongly that being in business for myself must be the key. Achieving success via higher education was tempting me. I worked closely with doctors, and that profession was of interest; however, the time commitment in getting there and a doctor's schedule was discouraging to me. I got my paramedic's license and went to work for an ambulance company making $17,300 a year. The money was not enough and the hours were demanding, even though I enjoyed the work of helping others.

I started to focus my thoughts on the fact that I kept hearing about people who were successful at investing in real estate. I was intrigued. So I took a real estate course and got my license.

I went to work part time for a typical real estate brokerage office. I asked the broker about investing, he said *"just focus on listing, the investing will come later"* I did not want to wait for later.

I saw an article on the front page of the real estate section of the Chicago Tribune newspaper. It was about a man named Gary Furstenfeld. He was very successful at buying foreclosures. The article indicated he taught classes at a downtown learning center. I called them and asked for his phone number. When they would not give it to me, I asked them to call and ask his permission. They did, and he did, and I called him. I told him of my interest in buying properties, and if he would teach me, I could then duplicate his efforts. I would be willing to work for free for the opportunity to be around him and learn. He arranged an interview appointment with me. It lasted two hours.

I left my paramedic job and went to work 12 to 14 hours a day, 6 to 7 days a week for three months — for free! I was not paid a dime! However, the education that I got, — well, this old cliché sums it up, *"If you feed a man a fish, you feed him for a day. If you teach a man to fish, you feed him for life!"* Nothing was just handed to me; my hand was not held. I pushed and shoved, asked for direction, and made things happen.

I share this bit of personal history with you in an attempt to instill in you the concept that you do not need money to get started in this business; nor do you need a great amount of education. You just need desire and the willingness to put forth the effort to make it happen. If you have money, it is just that much easier for you; however, the amount you have limits the amount you can do. The following can work for you as well as for the have not's.

No Money Down

The idea of "no money down" means no money out of your own pocket. It is called "O P M" — other people's money. For some of us, O P M is the only means for getting started in an investment program.

Creative financing as taught by some real estate enthusiasts is the method of buying real estate with "no money down." You contact sellers and negotiate with them to sign over their real estate to you without your having to put money up from your pocket. This is accomplished several different ways. Some examples are:

1. The seller plays the banker and finances the entire purchase. You just make monthly payments.
2. The seller agrees to use his credit to get an equity loan against the property so that he receives some cash from the property. Then he finances the purchase to you.

3. The seller agrees to sign over the property to you and allows you to refinance in your name and to get some cash out for him or the both of you.
4. The seller accepts from you some other asset as collateral in place of cash down. This could be a note secured against equity you have in another property.

There are many creative ways a deal could be structured.

You may be wondering why a seller would sell his real estate in such a creative / risky manner. There are several reasons. Here are some:

- Rough neighborhood — gangs, drugs, crime. He is tired of dealing with it!
- Financial pressure -

  — debt exceeds value; cannot sell it any other way.
  — it needs work, and the owner cannot afford to do it.
  — mis-management and or bad tenants.

You could probably buy properties like this all day long for no money down. However, you could end up putting money out of your pocket very quickly while dealing with the problems that the previous owner had. I believe the philosophy, "You get Nothing for nothing" is worthwhile. Or, "If it looks too good to be true, it probably is." Keep in mind that when someone wants to sell real estate, it takes some time and effort on their part. For them to invest that time and effort, there has to be some incentive. Either they need to have a monetary gain, or they need to get out of some liability.

"No Money Down" techniques have been taught by well-known and best selling authors. I am sure some people have made money with these techniques in dealing with "For Sale by Owners." I just believe, from my own experience, in focusing my time on the quickest and most profitable area of real estate investing. For me that has been foreclosures.

Creativity is the Key

The key element in working with foreclosures, or with little to no money, is **"Creativity."** It is having the mind set of finding ways to overcome difficulties. When faced with a stumbling block, it is not thinking, "OK, dead end; turn around and go back." It is finding a way to go over it, under it, around it, or right through it! It is not the lack of money that prevents one from achieving success in any endeavor. It is the lack of **creativity!**

The Reality of Real Estate Investing

Break out of pre-conceived notions that there is only one way to do things. Stretch your mind to new dimensions. Commit yourself to having a **"Positive Mental Attitude."** Have an **"I can do"** attitude! The antonym for "can" is no longer a part of your vocabulary. You can buy hundreds of thousands of dollars worth of real estate. I have done it. I have seen and helped others do it. So can you!

There are many sources for money, such as:

- **Credit cards for cash advances**
- **Lines of unsecured credit**
- **Banks for installment loans, secured and non-secured**
- **Partners**
- **Family or friends**
- **Paper money**
- **Credit Cards**

Used foolishly, the use of credit cards has sent many consumers to the bankruptcy court. However, used wisely, credit cards can help propel one to financial independence, even at 21%. Of course, you should always shop for your best credit card deal.

- Look for the lowest rate.
- Get a low or no annual fee.
- Get grace periods, especially on cash advances.
- Check the cash advance fees.

Whether you are starting with one card or several, develop an attitude that the purpose for these credit cards is for business. Any consumer charges are to be paid in full when the statement comes in.

If you already have cards, first inquire about credit line increases. Then choose the best three companies, fill out their applications, and send them off. In a week send off three more. Then wait.

As long as you have a somewhat decent credit and employment history and income, you will be approved. After the first two to four or five applications go through, then you will be denied for the reason of too many **recent** credit inquiries. That is OK; you have gotten started. With a denial of credit you have the right to a free copy of your credit report; so request it. When you have it exam it in detail, often there are minor mistakes and occasionally big mistakes. These mistakes are useful in helping to eliminate credit items you have that are negative. You dispute the item as being erroneous and damaging to your credit. It does not matter how small the mistake is, like a wrong date or balance on the account, if it is wrong it is erroneous. If the credit item is a negative item then it is certainly damaging to your credit. So dispute it. The credit bureau is then required by law to verify the correctness of the items. The hope then is that the creditor will not take the time or will not respond within the time limit. Then by law the credit bureau must remove the credit entry from your report. Usually within 30 to 40 days the credit bureau will send you a letter with their findings and the action taken. You then repeat the process with the remaining credit entries you want to pursue in having removed. In 2 to 3 months you send out your next set of applications and repeat that process.

Secure Card

If you are turned down due to negative credit items, then there is the secure credit card. This is where you deposit $100 - $500 - $1,000 in a savings account with a bank, and they extend you a credit line equal to two to three times your deposit amount. It is a start, and you build from there. There are other methods to clearing up, establishing, and rebuilding credit, far too extensive for this book. Go to the internet or your local library and research it.

Finance Companies

The interest rates of finance companies are a little higher. I have paid up to 23.9%. However, that was a pittance compared to the money I made from it. Some companies will even take an application from you over the phone and get back to you the same day with a credit line.

Banks

Some banks will do non-secured lines of credit or installment loans. Most prefer secured loans. When I was just starting to pursue my interest of gathering knowledge about investing in real estate, I refinanced my car to get $500 to attend a seminar. Anything of value can provide security for a loan — jewelry, vehicles, etc.

Establishing a relationship with a banker is a real plus. He can provide you with a quick refinance of an acquisition to free up money for your next purchase. However, if you are just starting out and have no assets nor a strong financial statement, then you will need to establish and cultivate a banker relationship. When you sit down with the bank's loan officer, let him know what your intentions are before you let him know of your meager beginnings. Let him know that you are a real estate investor and you wish to:

- ♦ Establish a relationship (which you realize may take some time) to be able to get quick loans against the equity in the real estate that you

acquire. The money you acquire would be for the purpose of remodeling and for additional acquisitions. Ask, is such a relationship possible?
- ♦ Know what their secured and non-secured lines of credit policies are.
- ♦ Know what terms they offer.
  – Origination fees? – Interest rate? – Length of the loan?

If you decide you are interested because you can see that the relationship has good potential, then open a saving's account with $500. Now make an application to borrow $500 using the savings account as collateral. That is an easy enough loan for the bank to make, and you are going to show the loan officer you are serious in getting started on this relationship. You may say the purpose of the loan is for business start up or equipment or for real estate acquisition. The loan officer's attitude may not be one of full confidence in your endeavor. However, you are setting out to prove yourself.

Now, you are not going to spend this money on any consumer purchases. You are going to find other banks and do it again three to five times. Eventually you will have the $500 parked in a savings account earning interest with no loan against it. The interest you are earning on each of the saving accounts will offset the interest you are paying on the loans. This technique has minimal cost and is an excellent way to get started with a good foundation to build upon. Keep in touch with each of your loan officers. Let them know of your successes and that you will eventually be bringing some more business their way.

Sources for Active Investors

Partners

A partner can be anyone with cash or credit available for you to use. Seek one that is passive — an armchair investor who just provides the money. He does not get actively involved in the deal itself.

A passive investor is anyone with money who would be interested in just earning a good rate of return. In general conversation you ask, *"Would you ever consider* an investment where your money would be secured against real estate with equity, where you *could earn an annualized 20% rate of return and a $1,000 origination fee? If an opportunity like that came your way would it be of interest to you?"*

Keep in mind you are not asking them to do so right now. You are taking mental notes for future reference. Then once you have located a deal and have all the particulars, you present it to them. See Case in Point # 1, Harlem Ave.

I prefer this kind of investor because he is not actively involved in the deal. You take the money, and you make the decisions. You do not take any profit until you close on a refinance or sale and pay your investor first. **Integrity** is the most important asset you will ever possess. The title of the property can go in the name of your investor or yourself — in which case you would sign a mortgage note. Depending on how well I know or trust my investors, or they know or trust me, sometimes ownership is 100% in their name, sometimes 100% my name, other times 50 / 50. Provide regular reports on how the deal is progressing and how you are spending the money. Always lean toward protecting your investor and making him feel comfortable. This is invaluable!

Now that I have achieved a good level of success I also act as what I refer to as a semi-passive investor to others who chase down deals. I say semi because I can not help but get a little involved.

- Seminars - There are usually some sort of investment seminars going on. Whether it is for real estate, mutual funds, stocks, etc., there are people with money looking to invest.
- Classified Ads "I Pay CASH For Homes" - These can usually be found in your local newspaper.
- Investment Clubs.
- Auctions.
- Your accountant, lawyer, insurance agent, doctor, or dentist.

There are always people out there with money to invest who lack the time or knowledge to invest it properly. Find them! They would love to earn the kind of rate of return you can offer secured against real estate with equity.

Most investors are eager to hear about a deal. They are also interested in making as much profit as they can. You will have to negotiate your profit. My best-structured deals were where I did everything — research, acquisition, management, marketing, and selling. The investors provided all the money for the acquisition, holding cost, remodeling, and marketing costs. We would then split the net profits 50 / 50 upon the closing of the sale. Or, I would offer them a guaranteed annualized 20% rate of return with a $1,000 origination fee. There was nothing paid until the closing of a refinance or a resell of the property. I preferred the guarantee rate method because it meant more money for me.

Family and Friends

To avoid negative input to your aspirations of investing, I recommend not even discussing it with those you are close to unless you know their thinking is on the same wave length as yours. They tend to be more critical. You do not need to hear criticism. You need to stay positive and focused.

Paper Money Techniques

Paper money is the technique of creating a note, trust deed, or mortgage to pay a sum of money to a seller. This can be secured against the real estate you are buying. This is most typical. Or, it can be against equity you have in any other real estate. It can simply be non-secured, a personal note, or secured against other personal property like a car. Use your creativity!

When creating a deal that involves owner financing, contract for deed, articles of agreement etc. You need to be sure and structure it so that you maintain a positive cash flow, while at the same time meeting the sellers needs. Sometimes it takes a little creativity.

- **Seasonal Adjusting Payment:** During the winter months you have a heating bill (an apartment building, for example) as an additional expense. The payments can be structured to be lower during this period so that the increased expense does not eat into your monthly cash flow.
- **Balloon Payments:** This technique can be used several ways.
   - Lower monthly payments and a lump sum (balloon) payment at the end of the financing period.
   - A small monthly payment and balloon payments quarterly, bi-annually, or annually.
   - No monthly payments, however quarterly, bi-annual, annual, or just one balloon payment at the end of the financing period.
- **Blanket Mortgage:** This is the technique of securing a note against not just one property but two or more. It is used when it is necessary to make a seller feel more comfortable with your deal. It is also a way of making small equities in property work for you that would otherwise just be sitting there anyway. The blanket does not need to run the whole term of the note. It can be six months or a year, just long enough for you to prove yourself to the seller. Then you have it automatically released.
- **The interest rate:** Can be worked with creatively, like the adjustable interest rate, where it starts lower and increases with certain limitations over the life of the loan. You could structure the loan to be interest payments only every three months.

Everything hinges on the circumstances both with the property itself and the seller. A moratorium (see glossary of real estate terms) can even be used, as with Case in Point # 13, 76 Units. That is why it is always important to establish rapport and get to know your seller's needs.

If the seller is still concerned about his security, you can buy a term-life insurance policy with a face value equivalent to the mortgage, and name the seller as the beneficiary. If you die, his note will be paid off in full. Your family will also be better off financially to be clear of the note. The cost for term-life insurance for the amount of your mortgage is very reasonable and worth using when necessary to get a deal done. You can buy property using equity in other property for part or all of your down payment.

First Right of Refusal

A clause that you should include in any note you create is the "First Right of Refusal." In the event the seller should consider selling his note in the future for a lump sum of cash, you get the first option to buy him out. People sell notes all the time, although not for face value. It is always at a discounted amount. If you happen to have the cash, it can be well worth paying it off for a discounted amount.

Financial Resume Profile

Once you have your first deal under your belt, you should buy a quality photo album and put together your portfolio to add to your financial resume profile folder. Now you can present your second deal a little more professionally with evidence that you have done it before. It is hard for someone to say something cannot be done when you have already done it, and you have the evidence to prove it.

A financial resume profile is basically a financial statement with all the documents to back you up. Any time you apply for a loan, they have you fill out a financial statement form. Then they will ask you to bring in certain documents, and they will send out verifications for some of the items you put on the statement. I say why not save time and make a great impression! Bring in everything they could possibly ask for, professionally organized in a folder that you can pick up from an office supply store. In it you will organize things like the following:

- Signed copies of your last two years of income tax returns.
- Last three pay stubs.
- Last three months of checking and savings account statements.
- Recent statements of all other financial assets.

The Reality of Real Estate Investing

- Itemized list of all real estate owned, including the address, year acquired, purchase price, name of mortgagee, mortgage balance, amount of monthly payment, current value, rental amount, amount of annual taxes, total of other hard monthly expenses (such as utilities and insurance), and in the far right column — the net monthly cash flow. At the bottom of the page, in the far right column, put the total monthly cash flow.
- Copies of all leases and insurance policies in the same order as the addresses. If there is no mortgage, include a copy of the deed.
- Copies of title or finance notes for all automobiles.
- If divorced, a copy of the divorce decree, child support order, etc.
- Documents to verify any other assets or liabilities.

This folder must be organized in a neat, orderly manner. When you present this to the loan officer and as he is overcoming his shock at how well-organized and prepared you are, ask him if he would have his assistant make a copy of the documents he needs while you wait. You should have each page of each section numbered with the small circular self-stick tabs. This will help the loan officer's assistant save time and help prevent a mistake when putting the documents back in the folder.

Keep all your information updated. You may even include the last credit report you have on yourself. By doing so you may be able to avoid another inquiry on your credit report.

Mortgage Hunting Tips

For those building up their available cash as I was, **"leverage"** is the name of the game. Get money, acquire a property, get the money back plus a profit, (it is a tax free profit when it is a refinance because it is borrowed) and do it again. On the properties you acquire and decide are keepers, because you have determined they have cash back value through a refinance and monthly positive cash flow value, long term financing becomes a factor. Important questions to consider when hunting for a mortgage are:

- **Do they allow cash back?**
- **Is there a minimum time ownership limitation?**
- **Are they a portfolio lender?**
- **What is their loan-to-value ratio?**
- **What are the non-owner occupant terms?**
- **What is the application fee?** — the interest rate? — points? — length of amortization?

Cash Back

Cash back means if you paid $20,000 for a house and want to re-finance it for 70% of value and it is worth $60,000, that is a new loan for $42,000 or $22,000 more than you paid for it. OK, let us say you spent $12,000 in fix-up; that still leaves $10,000. However, I have bought and refinanced some without having to do any repairs. See Case in Point # 16, 96th Pl. Now that $10,000 you have left over from the loan, after paying off the $32,000 in credit card advances, minus $1,000 in interest and loan fees, leaves you $9,000. That is to put in your pocket. It is **tax free** because it is borrowed money. You also have $18,000 in equity and a positive cash flow from the rent, because in your initial analysis you determined after P.I.T.I. (Principle, Interest, Taxes, Insurance), it would be there. Back to the cash back, that $9,000 is what a lender considers cash back. Some will allow it; some will not. Of course you want it. Some lenders will loan 70% - 80% of the appraised value; some will only loan 70% - 80% of the amount of money you have put into the deal.

Time Ownership Limitation

Some lenders want you to have owned a property for at least six months or a year before they will allow a refinance or cash back. Keep looking till you find one with out this limitation.

Portfolio Lender

To have a portfolio lender means they keep the loan "in house" within their control. They do not sell the loan on the secondary market. This is important to know because they decide their lending criteria and can make as many portfolio loans as they want. Loans that are sold on the secondary market have to follow strict governmental guidelines. Once you have three to five mortgages in your name, it becomes tougher to qualify for a loan that is to be sold on the secondary market. I have had up to nine 30 and 40 year mortgages from one portfolio lender at one time.

Loan to Value Ratio

Some lenders will only loan 50% or 60% of a property's value to an investor or non-owner occupant. You want to deal with lenders who will loan 70% - 80% or more, of the value so that you maximize your leverage position.

Terms

Non-owner occupant terms are always higher than owner occupant terms. The interest rate is usually about 2% more. That is a significant amount over thirty years. Of course, where does it say an owner has to occupy a house with an owner occupied loan for any specific amount of time? It does not. If your life situation allows you to move around a bit, you can take advantage of that lower rate.

The other fees associated with the loan, application fee, and points vary from lender to lender. You should shop for the best deal as you would for anything else.

Amortization

Amortization is the number of months and years you will pay back the loan. Most commonly you will hear about fifteen and thirty year mortgages. Different people have different philosophies on amortization. I think you should try to get the greatest number of years you can to pay back the loan. Then you have the lowest possible monthly mortgage payment obligation. You can always pay more if you want to reduce the number of years and the total interest you pay. However, if you ever have a tight month, you can pay the minimum. I feel this gives you more control and flexibility.

Walk Away Power

Remember your main objective as you structure your creative deals is to maintain a positive cash flow. If you find that is not possible, have walk-away power! Do not allow your emotions to cause you to be eaten alive. You see, whether you are standing in the middle of a swamp with an alligator chomping at your heels, or you own a building that is taking money out of your pocket every month, it is the same. You are about to be eaten alive! There are plenty of good deals to be made out there. Therefore, whether you are dealing with a seller or a lender, maintain your walk-away power!

Make the mistakes of yesterday your lessons for today.

CHAPTER 9

Successful Tenant Management

Real estate is a people business. As in any business with customers and clients, you treat them with friendliness and respect. Tenants and contractors are no different except you throw in a firm business-like manner with a pinch of compassion. For some people it is quite an ego trip to own property and be a landlord. OK, I will admit it is for me, too; however, my advice is to contain your ego. Represent yourself as a manager for the owner. It is much easier to say no as a middle person. You cannot be confronted directly. Tenants will say things to a sympathetic manager that they would not say to the owner.

Tenant / Landlord Relations

Acquiring and keeping good tenants is the key to success. Quick turnovers are costly and time consuming. Successful tenant management and minimizing turnovers is accomplished by maintaining a good relationship with your tenants. Develop a strong relationship by keeping your tenants satisfied. Some hints for doing this are:

- Remember that a good business relationship is based on mutual respect.
- Show an interest in their lives and needs.
- Keep your word! The fastest way to earn disrespect and loss of credibility is by not following up on your word. Take care of repairs and decorating as you have stated. Do not offer something you cannot or do not plan to deliver.
- Refer to your tenants as residents and as Mr. and Mrs.
- Give residents phone numbers to use in case of emergencies. I give them my office number since it is a real estate business and my cell phone number. It has voice mail and alerts me when I have a message, it also has caller ID in case I do not want to answer at that specific moment. If there is a problem with one of my properties, I want to know about it right away. I then call the appropriate person to go and take care of the problem. Also, give them a list of other important local emergency numbers including Police, Fire, Ambulance, etc.

- Respond promptly to requests for service. Even if you cannot meet their demands, let them know where you stand on the issue. Communication is the key to maintaining good tenant relations.
- Let residents know in advance what they can expect from you and what you expect from them on items such as rent payment, lease provisions, pets, complaints, services, etc.
- Respect their right to privacy and peaceful possession of their home. Give notice and make an appointment when you need to inspect their unit.

Determining Rent Amount

Just as with determining the value of a home, determining rental value is no exact science. Of course, the nicer your home appears, the more desirable it will be and the higher rent a tenant is willing to pay. The local newspaper is a good source to see what other homes in the area are renting for. Making appointments and going to see what the other homes look like and have to offer is an excellent way to become familiar with the market. Talk with other people in the area who may be renting or own rentals in the area.

Realtors can sometimes be helpful; however, selling, not rentals, is their focus. Rental agencies would be a good source since rentals are their focus. They should have a good data base of information as a resource for you.

The bottom line is to use your best judgment from the information you have acquired and put an amount on your home. Keep in mind that you can always adjust down, but not up. Some people like to set the amount $5 lower than the closest round number, for example $695 instead of $700. Which sounds better to you?

Finding a Tenant

A yard sign or window sign has produced a good, quick tenant for me many times. I put the sign up as soon as I have possession, or even before, depending on the circumstances. I do not feel it is necessary to wait until I have all the work completed and the home in perfect condition. The fact of the matter is that the tenant looking today or this week will have found a home by tomorrow or next week. They would not even have been a possibility for my home if I did not make it available. It is true that they will need to have a little imagination to visualize the home with the work completed. You, of course, help them to visualize by talking up the work that you are doing. If they still cannot visualize, oh well, you tried. However, most are able to visualize. The sooner you have a tenant lined up, the better. You will push harder to get the work done sooner. The quicker you get a tenant, the more money you save and earn.

Talk with the neighbors; become friendly with them. They are generally good security at helping to keep an eye on your property. Give them your name and telephone number. After all, they have somewhat of an invested interest in the homes surrounding theirs. They generally are not too excited about the prospect of your renting out the home. They would rather have a homeowner next door. However, if they know of someone who they feel would be a responsible tenant, they will be sure to refer that person to you.

You should also contact rental agencies in the area to make them aware of your property. Their service is usually at no charge to you; they charge the tenant. There are also bulletin boards in public locations, such as grocery stores or the Internet, where you can put up a flyer. Last, but not least, are the classified ads in the newspaper. This usually produces the most leads.

Screening Tenants

You want to be prepared with some questions to pre-screen the callers from your for rent advertisement. That way you invest your time with only good candidates when meeting them face to face. Have your questions prepared and written out ahead of time on one page. Have another page where you have drawn lines to make columns for each lead's name, phone number and answers. This is the best way to keep track and to remember them. Sometimes the calls come in fast and furious. If prospective tenants are hesitant or refuse to cooperate in answering your questions, eliminate them. They just saved you some time and probably money, too.

Section 8 Tenants

Section 8 tenants are government subsidized tenants, for part or all of their rent payments. I like the program because the rent checks come every month just like clock work. You still screen the tenants because there are good and bad within the Section 8 program, just as with everything else.

Disabled Tenants

My wife and I having a disabled son and thinking of his future housing needs, and helping a good friend that is disabled and in need of housing, began a new direction for us. We founded the

The Reality of Real Estate Investing

"**Housing Resource Center, Inc.**". A not for profit organization with a focus on providing housing for disabled people and other related assistance. We have learned that there is a big need in this area. People with disabilities seem to be discriminated against. I am sure it is just due to lack of knowledge and understanding. Screened properly as always, disabled people make great tenants. Some are on Section 8 as well, most have fixed incomes; disability, social security, pensions and some also work. Not all disabled people are in wheel chairs, some are blind, deaf, back problems, on oxygen 24 hours a day, cerebral palsy, downs syndrome and a host of other reasons. Even those in wheel chairs have value as a tenant for the right home. Making the home assessable is not difficult or costly, sometimes grants are available to help with the alterations. Also, the disabled person in the family is not always the adult or breadwinner, sometimes it is one of the children.

Once disabled people have a place to live that is suitable for their needs they tend to not want to move again. Low turnover is a real positive! For more information go to the Hot Links page on my web site **www.HomeBargains.com**.

Questions To Ask

- How many adults and children are in your family that would be occupying the home / apartment? What are the children's ages? A large number of children is not necessarily a negative. One of my best tenants had nine children. See Case in Point # 2, Hoyne.
- What are your sources of income?
- What are your debts?
- Where do you live now?
- Why are you moving?
- Do you have any negative marks on your credit report?

Let them feel you are going to pull a credit report even if you are not. I recommend you have your final candidates provide you with a current copy of their credit report. Provide them with the information they will need to order it themselves and how much it will cost. An alternative to this is to establish a relationship with a loan officer, such as the one you use or will use for your mortgages. Their companies are hooked up to the credit bureau. The loan officer can pull up a credit report quickly for you and without cost. Also, there are "for pay" services available. Besides providing a credit report, they also do a judgment search to see if the tenant has ever had a rental or any other kind of a judgment against them. Check the Hot Links page on my web site for a source that I use.

- Have you ever been evicted or taken to court over a rent dispute? Of course, if they have, most will lie about it. However, if they are bold enough to say yes, for whatever reason, perhaps they felt they were justified in their dispute with the landlord. Regardless, you do not want them. They are now savvy to how the process works. It will be more hassle and take longer to evict them. The credit report may also reflect a prior eviction or rental money judgment.

For Section 8 tenants:

- Ask the same questions as above.
- How many bedrooms are you qualified for?
- The amount of rent section 8 pays is based on the number of bedrooms the tenant is qualified for, which is based on the number of children in the family.
- What is their source of income; public aid, food stamps, child support, a job?
- Ask if they are going to school?
- When presenting as a single mom, ask if the father of children or another male person, sometimes it is a brother, comes around and sometimes stays over?

You will find that a male person sometimes lives with them all the time. Section 8 just does not know about them. I actually view this as a positive because the family has more of a support system. And the male person can help out around the home with mowing grass, shoveling snow etc.

I will also mention here that I do not rent to unrelated couples who are not married who just want to shack up. Besides the main reason of it not being morally correct, it is a high risk situation for a landlord. There is not sufficient commitment in the relationship to weather the storms. Those who are married understand what I mean. Any relationship has ups and downs, disagreements, arguments etc. Shack up situations make it easy for one person to just pack up and take off in a heated rush. The person left behind may not be able, or want to pay rent anymore. Now you have a problem!

When you have two males or two females wanting to become roommates and rent from you include the following sentence in the lease.

"Each lessee is responsible for the entire lease individually. "

Once you have the answers to your questions, you can tell the prospective tenants you will pass this information on to the owner and you will get back to them if he is interested. Or, if you already know that you are interested, you may go ahead and set an appointment. To maximize the use of your time, schedule a

The Reality of Real Estate Investing

couple or several appointments five to ten minutes apart. Expect the fact that you will have some no shows.

When you are face to face, listen! If you are naturally a talkative person, control yourself. You learn more from listening than talking. Of course, you should always have a friendly demeanor. Keep in mind you are about to decide who you are going to entrust with your valuable asset. This is your money machine. The last thing you need is a tenant who presents himself as an angel and then transforms into the tenant from hell who turns your home into a money eating alligator.

You bought this book for the information it contains to help you earn and save money. Take my advice to heart. If you do otherwise, you will end up with money out of your pocket a hundred times the cost of this book. It indeed will be an expensive lesson. I am trying to emphasize this point because I know; I have made the mistakes! Those mistakes have cost me plenty.

After giving prospective tenants a tour through the home and you have decided you are interested in them so far, and if they have not already indicated so, ask them if they are interested in the home. If they respond positively, ask them if they would like to fill out an application. Hand them an application; you would prefer they fill it out right then at the counter or in the car. If they want to take it with them, let them know they could fax it back to you to save time. You do not want to be waiting around a couple of days for a good prospective tenant to get back to you if you can avoid it. Let them know they may not be the only tenant for the owner to consider, that you like them, and would like to see them get the home.

If you actually have to pay to get a copy of their credit report, that cost will be their application fee. Offer to provide them a copy of their credit report for review. Also, tell your prospective tenants that a deposit of $50 - $100 minimum with the application is necessary to show their seriousness, and it will be applied toward their security deposit. If they are hesitant about this, you have to question their serious intent to take the home. Some will be willing to give the full amount and the first month's rent right then in cash. Do not let this tactic intimidate you. Check them out in the normal procedure. You would not want to take their money if you did not feel good about them getting the home because you do not like handling other people's money or the hassle of refunding it.

Once you know that you do not want the tenant, quickly show them through and talk as little as possible. Say good-bye to them at the door. For those who express their interest in the home, I do not advise you to tell them you are not interested in them. Be tactful. If they ask for an application, it is best to give them one. Avoid any problems. You will just never call them back. If they call you, tell them the owner decided on someone else.

Playing Detective

Once you have the application and deposit, your next step is to start confirming your first impression. If everything appears good on the application and their credit report, you are now going to call their current landlord. You are not going to tell him you are interested in renting your home to his tenant. You are going to contact the current landlord under the guise of being a used car salesperson. I know it is sneaky and it is tricky; but think about it. How else are you going to get the truth? If the current landlord has a tenant who owes a couple months' rent and has trashed his home or apartment, do you think he is going to tell you this so it ensures they stay in his unit longer? Not likely. He will be telling you how great this tenant is so that you help get them out of his property. Understand now? Sometimes in life we have to be a little sneaky and tricky to get to the truth.

Basically you say something like, "*Hi! My name is _____ with A & W Used Auto Sales. I have an application here from (prospective tenant's name) to finance a used car. Could you verify for me that ____ pays the rent on time?*" If the tenant does owe this landlord money, he is going to think, "*This jerk owes me money and is trying to use me as a reference to finance a used car!*" There is no way the landlord is going to give a good reference. If it is bad, you might have to interrupt to tell him you have heard enough. However, if it is good, you can be reasonably assured it is the truth.

In-Home Inspection

Your next step in determining if you should take a risk with this tenant is to show up unexpectedly at their front door. You could say something like, "*The owner has narrowed the selection down to two people, and you are one of them. I just wanted to drop off a copy of the lease for you to look over.*" Then you say, "*Could I trouble you to use your rest room (or phone)?*" Nine times out of ten this will get you in. If they resist because they say the house is a mess, reassure them that it is OK; you can see past day-to-day clutter. Start to enter. You have to be a tad bit aggressive here. Your time is wasted if you do not get in. If they still resist, then own up to the fact that the owner requires you to get a quick look at the condition of the home / apartment they presently live in. If they do not let you in, for sure the owner will not accept them. Again reassure them you can see past the day-to-day clutter.

Once inside, you are looking for long term filth, dirty walls, doors, and floors, holes in the walls and doors, dirty clothes over the floor in the hallway or bath and you can hardly avoid walking on them, garbage and food where it should not be, animal odor or feces on the floor. I have literally been in a home where I had to watch where I was stepping to avoid feces and urine puddles from the dog or cat. It was unbelievable! Was I ever thankful that I did an inspection! Do roaches exist in the home? If so, is it a heavy infestation? I have seen where they were crawling on the ceiling, and I had to be careful not to walk under them. Talk about creepy! You can get a sense if people are comfortable with roaches as just part of the family, or if it is a problem they are struggling to be rid of. However, understand roaches move with the family. There is no way to avoid it!

Measures can be taken to annihilate roaches over a thirty to sixty day time period. Tell the tenants that prior to packing up their stuff to move, you want them to set off a smoke bomb in every room. Smoke bombs can be acquired at most building supply stores. This will get rid of most of them but not the unhatched eggs. For the rest and the eggs that will hatch in your property, there is a paste formula that can be acquired via the hot links page on my web site **www.HomeBargains.com**. I have used it for years when necessary. It never fails to succeed at total annihilation.

Over all, use basic common sense when inspecting the prospective tenant's home and always be courteous. When leaving, tell them you will get back to them as soon as you can. Do so later that day or the following morning. If you have decided to take them, invite them into your office. If you do not have an office, return to their home or have them meet you at the rental property. Remind them that they will need to bring their first month's rent and the balance of the security deposit with them.

Security Deposit

Require the first month's rent and a security deposit equal to the amount of two months' rent. When you first tell them this, follow up immediately with this question, *"Is that workable for you?"* If they hesitate or indicate that it is not, and reasonably so because it is a great amount of money on top of moving expenses, you could indicate that perhaps payments on the second month could be acceptable. When you sit down for the signing of the lease, a collection of the balance of the money and an agreement on payments are necessary. Write the payment plan on the lease and be specific. You will be glad you stuck to this requirement some day when a good tenant goes bad.

When a tenant wants to move in during the middle of the month, you simply pro-rate the daily rent, still collect the full first months' rent and credit the second months' rent with the partial months' credit. I have been known to just give a few days for free when tenants are moving in towards the end of the month.

The Rental Agreement

A standard rental application and lease agreement can be acquired at your local office supply store. I am going to focus on **riders** to the lease agreement. Copies of these are enclosed at the end of the chapter. It is a good gesture to provide your tenants with twelve (12) pre-addressed envelopes to pay their rent.

Move-in Inspection

If you have ever rented a moving truck, you will remember that the company had you do an initial inspection and mark on a form any scratches or dents you noticed. You are going to have your tenant do a similar thing prior to moving in.

Item # 18 in the Resident Policy and Regulation form covers the condition of the home or apartment, and allows space for any damages to be noted. For example; a stain or burn on the carpet, vinyl flooring, cabinets, counters, etc. Never point out items you notice, let the tenant point them out. If you start pointing things out the tenant might start asking you to replace a counter because there is a scratch on it. The purpose of this is so you can justly require them to pay for damages (which would be deducted from the security deposit) upon their move out, and to encourage them to be mindful of taking care of the residence and keeping damages to a minimum.

Resident Policy & Regulations
(as they appropriately apply)

ATTACHED TO AND MADE PART OF LEASE AGREEMENT DATED_____.

1. Rent three (3) or more days late is grounds for immediate eviction. Non-sufficient funds checks are deemed as rent not being paid. On-time rent discount is forfeited and there is a $25 non-sufficient funds charge.

2. Lessee will receive a discount off rent when paid by the first of the month.

3. Lessee acknowledges Lessor's recommendation to acquire renter's insurance.

4. Any resident engaging in or allowing criminal activity (including drug-related criminal activity) will be referred to the proper authorities for prosecution and will be immediately evicted.

5. Only residents named on the lease are allowed to live in the residence. Over-night guests are limited to two (2) persons and stays are limited to two (2)

nights unless previously authorized by management. Each resident will be responsible for the actions of guests, friends, or visitors.

6. Noisy, disorderly or offensive conduct, or conduct annoying or disturbing to other residents shall be grounds for termination of occupancy. Radios, TV's, and stereos must be kept at low volume between the hours of 10:00 P.M. and 8:00 A.M.

7. Pets are prohibited in the buildings or on the grounds at any time.

8. The laundry facilities are for the convenience of the residents and must be left clean after each use.

9. All refuse must be placed in the garbage containers provided. No garbage should be placed outside the doors of the unit. Residents shall not discard cigarettes or other litter on the property grounds.

10. Signs, advertisements, or notices shall not be painted or affixed upon any part of the building, outside or inside; nor shall any article be suspended outside the buildings or placed on the window sills.

11. Upon proper advance notice, resident will grant access to the residence for the purpose of pest control. This will be carried out under management supervision.

12. Lessee acknowledges that the premises presently have no signs of roaches or rodents and is responsible to keep it that way.

13. Tenants must receive permission from management in order to: install wall anchors; remodel; paint the interior; or attach any fixtures to walls, floor, or ceilings.

14. Sidewalks, driveways, passages, and common areas shall not be obstructed or used for any other purpose than entrance and exit from the residence, unless otherwise designated. This is required by local ordinance fire code. Chairs must be removed from walkways and areas in front of the residence immediately after use.

15. Use of any parking area other than that assigned for parking is prohibited. Car washing or maintenance requiring more than two (2) hours is prohibited in any area. Cars parked in no-parking areas, as well as inoperable or abandoned cars, will be subject to tow-away procedures.

16. <u>Housekeeping:</u> Tenants are expected to keep their residence clean and undamaged.

17. Lessee is responsible for routine maintenance and upkeep. Lessee shall vacuum the carpet often, shampoo the carpet at least once every six (6) months, and shall provide receipts to lessor as proof.

18. Lessee acknowledges that there are no holes in the walls or doors or any other damages, that the residence is in a good, clean condition. Lessee agrees to return it in the same condition. If there are any areas within the residence with damage, it should be noted here: _____

19. <u>Miscellaneous Tenant Charges:</u>

    Mini-blinds replacement: $ 35
    Screen replacement: $ 25
    Window single pane replacement: $ 50
    All keys: $ 5

20. The Security Deposit will not be used in place of rent.

21. Upon termination of the lease it will convert automatically to a month-to-month lease, unless other arrangements are made. A 30-day written notice is required prior to moving. If the resident fails to turn over possession by the last day of the lease period when moving, the possession hold-back rental rate will be equal to one and a half times the resident's prior daily rental amount.

LESSEE AGREES TO REPORT <u>ALL</u> PROBLEMS TO MANAGEMENT IMMEDIATELY!

I have read and agree to abide by the above policies.

_____   _____
    Lessee   Date   Lessor   Date

Concerning # 2 above: Of course, the discount is really not a discount at all. If you advertised your apartment or home for $600 a month, you add $50 or $100 to it when you fill out the lease. At first glance the tenants will be surprised. You quickly explain they are getting a discount. It is $600 a month as long as they pay by the first of the month. Then say, "*You do intend to pay your rent on time, right?*" If they have a problem, then explain that the owner feels if they are not willing to accept this, they are basically saying they plan to pay late. Then they will sign. If properly enforced, this makes paying rent on time a big priority. One of my students consistently had one of his tenants paying late. The on-time rent was discounted $75, but the tenant paid the extra $75 each month. I suppose I would not mind getting the rent later in the month for an extra $75.

Concerning # 3 above: This is an important clause. Should a fire, theft, or flood occur on your property, whether it is the tenants' fault or not, the tenants will assume that your insurance should pay for their loss. Recommend they acquire renter's insurance because your insurance only covers the home or building. Their personal property is not covered by your policy.

Concerning # 16 and # 17 above: The tenant must take responsibility for upkeep and practice good housekeeping skills. Of course, performing the surprise inspection of their prior residence is the best test.

Concerning # 21 above: This gives you the flexibility of having a month-to-month agreement after one (1) year in the event you are thinking of selling or you simply forget to prepare a new lease on time. If you desire to keep the tenant for another year, send the renewal lease sixty (60) days prior to the lease expiration. This puts your tenants on notice that you are expecting another year lease at an increased rental of $10 per month or what your market currently justifies. If they are going to move then it gives you time to find a new tenant. You want to encourage and provide incentive for move-outs on the agreed upon date or sooner. Your next tenant may be ready to move right in.

When Tenants Go Bad

Regardless of how well you screen your tenants, you will one day be faced with performing an eviction. Even when tenants have been screened very well, circumstances of life will happen to them. Couples split up, people have medical problems, jobs are lost, and on and on. It is not really what happens to us that makes the difference. It is how we respond! Some people are able to pull themselves up by their boot straps and do what they need to do. Others become paralyzed, unable to act, or refuse to do so. Some think everyone else owes them, to help them maintain what they currently have instead of sacrificing and doing without until they are able to build themselves back up again. Granted, if you have the means, there is nothing wrong with helping a fellow human being out. However, it should not be to the point where they are taking advantage of you or not utilizing their own resources. At that point it is time to evict.

My advice is that when there has been no communication about a rent payment being late, on the fourth day serve the 5-day notice (or as is appropriate for your area). Enforce the full rent, and do not allow the normal on time discount. You have to set a precedent. If you let them off, they will feel you are not serious about paying the rent on time, and they will not make paying their rent as much of a priority.

If at the end of the 5-day notice period the tenant has not made appropriate arrangements, then proceed with the filing of the eviction. You could wait; however, each day that goes by is costing you money!

I do recommend your getting advice from your attorney on the legal procedures for your area. You want to be sure to follow them exactly. There is nothing worse than having a judge throw your case out on a minor technicality and you have to start all over. Then the tenant goes strolling out of court with a big smile on his face, and you realize that he is going to take you for at least another month's worth of rent. Do your homework! If you can afford it, you can hire an attorney to perform the entire process. I think it is worthwhile to do it yourself at least once for the experience.

Get your judgment and order of possession. In Illinois the judge will usually stay the possession order for seven plus days (which means postpone), depending on the number of occupants. Then you can file and pay the sheriff to perform the eviction. The cost is about $225 and rising for the sheriff. During the stay period I make a business decision. I approach the tenant and offer him "Cash for Keys" - $100 or so to go ahead and move out. After all, he knows he must go, either on his own or with the assistance of the sheriff. It will cost me more with the sheriff. Even though he owes me money, I will pay him to go ahead and move. The other part of the equation is that it may be two, three, or four weeks before the sheriff comes out after I file. Therefore, I save time, also. If he accepts, I am that much ahead of the game. Sure you will struggle with your emotions, but the bottom line is, it is the best business decision.

A condition of the "Cash for Keys" is they must be completely out with the unit broom-swept clean, and the tenant hands you the keys; then you hand him the money. **Make no exceptions!**

Concerning the money they owe, once you have a judgment you can do a wage assignment. I had one tenant who had changed jobs, and I did not know where he worked. I let it go and forgot about it. About three years later I got a phone call from the tenant. He had to refresh my memory who he was. He had just been pre-qualified for a mortgage to go home shopping. The only thing standing in his way was my rent judgment of $600. I made him a deal. I would call it even for $300 as long as he allowed me to be his Realtor on his home purchase. He agreed, and I earned a $1500 commission.

Insurance

Shortly after acquiring one of my properties and doing some interior clean out and prep work for remodeling, I was installing a new furnace and putting on a new roof. Since vandalism was a potential concern, I had one of the workers of the general contractor I had hired spending the night there. He was equipped with a cot, a small electric heater, and a television. The purpose of his staying there, of course, was for security.

I do not know what actually happened, but early one Sunday morning I got a phone call informing me that my property had burned down. When I arrived, it looked like a giant icicle since it was the middle of January in Chicago. The worker apparently was unharmed. He was gone, and we never heard from him again. The furnace, which was in the basement where there was no fire damage, had been stolen. The firemen determined that the fire had started from an electrical short in the second floor bedroom where the worker had been staying.

The insurance adjuster determined the repair cost at about $25,000 utilizing union wage contractors. I completed the rehab at about $19,000. The $6,000 left over was mine to put in my bank account.

On another property I was faced with an injury lawsuit. See Case in Point # 21, Avers. Obviously having proper fire and liability insurance paid off. Without it, I would have been devastated.

I am not going to attempt to teach you all there is to know about property insurance. I will leave that to your insurance agent. As with anything else you should shop around for the best deal. If you currently own a home, start with your home owner's insurance agent. Then call upon two or three more to compare rates and their recommendations for a landlord's policy.

Be sure to provide accurate information about the construction and square footage of your building. The premium you pay is partially based on this information. Mention any improvements or updates, such as new roofing, heating, plumbing, and electrical wiring. This information could significantly reduce your premiums.

You also want to choose a company with a Best rating of A or A+. This indicates an excellent financial condition and operating performance. Most mortgage companies require this.

There are two types of insurance agents. An "Independent Agent" represents many different insurance companies, like Hanover, Cigna, Kemper, Fireman's Fund, Travelers, Reliance, and Continental, to name a few. A "Direct Writer" typically represents one company, like Allstate, Farmers, or State Farm. Obtain quotes from both types for the best comparison.

Your agent should be insured for errors and omissions, and you should require proof of this coverage. This proof can be produced in the form of a certificate of insurance. You may have recourse under this coverage if your agent mistakenly fails to provide coverage for which you paid.

Property Taxes

The following discussion is intended to help you understand how your tax bills are calculated. Local laws may vary; consult your local tax office.

Market Value

The assessor, or assessor's appraiser, has the responsibility of determining a market value for each property in a jurisdiction (county, township, borough, or parish). The market value of a property is the price the property would probably sell for in a competitive market. If there has not been a recent sale of a property comparable to yours, the assessor uses other methods to determine a market value.

One method that would be used, especially on newer or special use buildings, is the cost approach, which determines the current cost of replacing the improvements, less depreciation from all causes, plus the value of the land.

Another method used for income producing property is the income approach. This establishes the value by capitalizing the income the property produces or is expected to produce.

Once the market value is decided, the assessed value can be determined.

Assessed Value

The assessed value is a percentage of the market value. It varies between states, within a state, and / or by type of property, and can be 100 percent of the market value. In Illinois the percentage used to determine the assessed value for residential rental properties is 33 1/3 percent of the market value. Therefore, an apartment building purchased for $150,000 would have an assessed value of $50,000. In Cook County, which consists of Chicago and many surrounding suburbs, there is one exception to this. Any apartment building with six units or less has an assessment value of 16 percent. Thus, a $150,000 six-flat located in Cook County would have an assessed value of $150,000 times 16 percent, or $24,000.

Equalization Factor

When the assessor determines market value and takes the proper percentage of that amount and computes an assessed value, the state injects a multiplier called the state equalization factor. This factor varies between counties. Many states outside Illinois do not have an equalization factor, and so the following would not apply.

According to the State of Illinois, the purpose of the multiplier is to make assessed values equitable between the counties. Comparable properties located in comparable areas in different counties should have approximately the same value. In an effort to keep the state factor, or multiplier, at one, a township may apply its own factor that covers only that township. However, a township factor does not preclude the state from applying a factor, also.

Tax Rate

Once you have an equalized assessed value, the tax rate (or in many states the millage rate) is determined. Local taxing bodies add up assessed value on all properties in their jurisdictions. The total operations budgeted amount is divided by the total assessed value base to determine the tax or millage rate. Multiplying the equalized assessed value by the tax or millage rate gives you your total taxes due (tax bill).

Are you Over-Assessed?

A property could be over-assessed (or under-assessed) even though the assessors have done their jobs properly. Assessors have many properties to assess at any given time; they tackle this problem by using a mass appraisal approach. The assessor takes comparable properties in comparable areas and places comparable market values and, therefore, comparable assessed values on them. Since the assessor is not inspecting properties for their unique features, the values they place are almost always inexact. An individual appraisal is much more accurate for determining market value because it focuses on the unique characteristics of the property.

When purchasing property, it is generally a good idea to allocate a portion of the purchase price for personal property that should be shown on the closing statement. Personal property is taxable in many states, but not in Illinois. If below-market financing is involved, the selling price may be inflated and, if so, it should be adjusted downward to reflect the effects of the financing. The assessed value should not indicate a market value higher than what was paid for the property after the adjustments for personal property and financing.

There may be comparable properties near your property that are assessed lower than your building. You will need photographs of these properties when you go in to the assessor with this information. The assessor may lower your assessed value or raise the assessed value on the comparable properties.

When using an income approach (rental property), keep in mind that assessors employ guidelines in determining normal operations of a property. They follow these guidelines when looking at vacancies, percentage of taxes to gross possible rent, and percentage of expenses to gross possible rent. For example, in Cook County the real estate taxes should not exceed twenty five percent of gross possible rent. In the rest of Illinois the guideline is fifteen percent of gross possible rent. For vacancies and expenses, guidelines vary with the neighborhood and size of the property.

If your vacancies or expenses are higher than the guidelines, it is up to you to prove that these problems should be considered in assessing the property and are not due to poor management. Assessors do not have to lower the value on a property simply because the owner or manager is not doing an adequate job. Be ready to justify and support your claims, especially major, unexpected, and necessary expenses. Be ready to give reasons why you are experiencing vacancies.

Anything that causes major damage to the property, such as flood, fire, tornado, and so on should be brought to the attention of the assessor. Any problem with the property that would have a negative effect on value should be documented.

Valuation and Tax Rate Protests

In many states property is reassessed every year. In Illinois, however, Cook County reassesses one quarter of its properties each year. The year that a property is scheduled to be reassessed is called the *quadrennial.* However, the taxpayer may file a complaint in any and every year, and the assessor can reassess the property in non- quadrennial years.

In Cook County the taxpayer files a complaint with the assessor's office. You do not need legal representation. The assessor's office has all the forms, and you supply whatever documentation is relevant to your case. The assessor then renders a decision.

If you are dissatisfied with this decision, you can proceed to the Cook County Board of Tax Appeals. From this point forward in Cook County, you must have legal counsel. Your attorney would file a petition with supporting documentation and argue the case.

After the Board of Tax Appeals, your attorney can file a Specific Objection Complaint (SOC) and / or a Certificate Of Error (COE). To file an SOC for the current year, the taxes must be paid on time, in full, and under protest. Also, a complaint must have been filed for the prior year's taxes with the Cook County Board of Tax Appeals, which was discussed above. Since an SOC is a lawsuit, it must be drafted by your legal counsel. No form is provided by the courts. The Circuit Court of Cook County will approve or disapprove the SOC.

When a certificate of error is filed for the current year, an assessed valuation complaint must be filed with the Assessor of Cook County for the upcoming year. The Board of Tax Appeals must approve the COE; thus, if they deny relief for the current year, they probably will not approve the COE. Therefore, your attorney would also file an SOC, which does not need approval of the Board of Tax Appeals.

In Illinois counties other than Cook, the system is different. You do not need an attorney to proceed with the complaint beyond the assessor's office. After the Assessor you can file a complaint with the Board of Review. If needed, you can then file with the Property Tax Appeal Board (PTAB). The PTAB is run by the state and handles complaints from all over the entire state except Cook County. Even though you do not need an attorney, you should hire one for this step in the appeal process, unless you are very knowledgeable.

In many states the appeal process is similar to the Illinois system, excluding Cook County. The names for the review boards vary between states as do the forms and the rigidity of the rules for filing. In many areas the assessors or appraisers are willing to work with a taxpayer to determine the value of the property before formally issuing a notice. By working with the assessor in this manner, you may be able to avoid the appeal process altogether. Check with the local office and / or with other taxpayers familiar with the appeal process in your area to determine the best course of action.

In Illinois when you pay taxes under protest, you are claiming that the tax rate is excessive. This means that the taxing districts have over budgeted and you have paid too much in taxes because the tax rate on your bill is too high. Paying taxes under protest is of benefit only if at least one law firm in your county analyzes the budgets of the various taxing districts and files in court for refunds based on the analysis.

There are law firms that specialize in doing this work in Cook County and several other counties surrounding Chicago. In these counties an attorney pays the taxes on your behalf, on time, and in full, but under protest. The process can sometimes be very long, possibly ten years or more in Cook County, before you receive a refund. The actual procedure for paying under protest consists of merely filling out a protest form and submitting it with your tax bill and check at the time of payment. In some areas there may also be a small fee.

Some other states also allow for payment under protest. Check with your local office for further details.

For More Information

If you have questions but are not quite ready to hire an attorney, there are several organizations that you can contact. One is the Illinois Property Assessment Institute (IPAI), 707 North East Street, Bloomington, IL 61701, (309) 828-5131. Other states also have their own state organizations. Another is the International Association of Assessing Officers (IAAO), 131 East 60th Street, Chicago, IL 60637-9990, (773) 947-2069. There is also the Institute of Property Taxation, 122 C Street NW, Suite 200, Washington, DC 20001, (202) 347-5115. These organizations offer classes and material concerning property taxation at reasonable fees. The Illinois Department of Revenue also has some helpful materials at a reasonable fee. Taxpayers in other states should call their own state offices to determine what materials are available and which department offers it.

If you do not have time to learn about property taxes, retain an attorney. Look for one who is established in the field, preferably one who works almost exclusively in the field of property taxes and has a reputation for being honest, reliable, and imaginative.

Bookkeeping

Keeping accurate records of your income and expenses is very important. This is necessary not only for the general operations of each of your properties but also for tax preparation and IRS audits.

I do not write on this subject as a Certified Bookkeeper or CPA, but just as an experienced Real Estate investor / landlord. When I first started, I had no formal training and still do not, except for the college of hard knocks. Trial and error served as my teacher. I set up a separate checking account for every property. I spent hours each month balancing the accounts. I would spend forty plus hours each year preparing spread sheets by long-hand with all the income and expenses itemized for my accountant. It was a nightmare! Now I do it all on a computer.

I am sure there are several software programs available for this purpose, but I am personally familiar with Quicken, which I like very much. With one checking account I enter the check number, to whom it was payable, the debit amount, and then I categorize it. For example, I own a home in Chicago Heights on Yorktown Road. Since this is the only home I own in Chicago Heights, I categorize this property as C-Hgts. If I owned two properties in Chicago Heights, I would probably call it Yorktown. It does not matter how you categorize it as long as you name it and know which property you are referring to.

Next, you name the sub-category (for example - "C-Hgts: Repair"). It could be advertising, utilities, legal, etc. The next entry is a space for a memo if you feel a comment is necessary. Deposits are also categorized (example - rent, security deposit, washer and dryer, Jones Unit 3, etc.).

Reconciliation is easy each month. Monthly, quarterly, bi-annual, and annual reports are a matter of pushing a couple of buttons. You can see exactly what has transpired with your property and what the net is. You give this report to your accountant, and he can easily prepare your taxes. Quick, simple, easy! Now you have more time to spend with the kids!

I have been audited by the IRS twice thus far in life. Therefore, I would like to share with you some more information. My comments on this subject are certainly not all-encompassing. However, my hope is that my comments on my personal experience serve as useful tips for you.

The IRS officer will be impressed with the nice looking organized report of all your income and expenses for each property. However, that will not be good enough. If you are sitting in front of an IRS officer, it is because he has questions about specific income or expenses on your return. He wants to see specific documentation to back up your claims or deductions. Therefore, you need a paper trail consisting of receipts or canceled checks. If you pay $30 to someone for doing some lawn maintenance and pay in cash, you should still write a check payable to that person and let him endorse it over to you. Write in the memo area "C-hgts: lawn maintenance." This completes a paper trail.

On utility stubs and other receipts write the check numbers on them. In case you ever need to refer to the check, you will already have the number to look for. Create separate, categorized legal size envelopes for storing the receipts and cancelled checks throughout the year. Keep them in a drawer or box in alphabetical order. This keeps you organized and saves you much time and many headaches.

Additional Riders for the Rental Agreement
Smoke Detector Agreement

This agreement is entered into this_____ day of _____ 20__, and made a part of the Rental Agreement by and between _____, Owner / Landlord, and _____, Resident.

OWNER AND RESIDENT AGREE AS FOLLOWS

1. Resident is renting from the owner the premises located at: _____.
2. The premises is equipped with a smoke detection device(s).
3. The resident acknowledges the smoke detector(s) was (were) tested and the operation explained by management in the presence of the Resident at the time of the initial occupancy and the detector(s) in the unit was (were) working properly at the time.
4. Each resident shall perform the manufacture's recommended test to determine if the smoke detector(s) is (are) operating properly at least once a week.
5. Initial on the line ONLY IF BATTERY OPERATED: _____. By initialing as provided, each Resident understands that said smoke detector(s) and alarm is a battery operated unit and it shall be each Resident's responsibility to:

   a. ensure that the battery is in operating condition at all times;
   b. replace the battery as needed; and
   c. if, after replacing the battery, the smoke detector(s) do not work, inform the owner or authorized agent immediately by phone and in writing.

6. Resident(s) must inform the owner or authorized agent immediately by phone and in writing of any defect, malfunction or failure of any detector(s).

_____   _____
     Owner / Agent   Resident

The following rider is useful if your a licensed agent. It gives incentive to tenants, to be good tenants and to utilize your services when deciding to buy a home.

If your not licensed, you can substitute the name of your favorite agent in exchange for the best favors you can negotiate.

RENT CREDIT PROGRAM REGISTRATION

Apply a portion of your annual rent to the purchase price of the home, condo, town home, or apartment building of your choice. Purchase this real estate anywhere in the United States.

Cash you will get at closing	When purchase price is:
$100	$ 0 - 55,000
275	55,001 to 70,000
350	70,001 to 85,000
425	85,001 to 100,000
500	100,001 to 115,000
575	115,001 to 130,000
650	130,001 to 145,000
725	145,001 or greater

Conditions

1. Sign a 12-month lease with one of the homes, condos, or apartment buildings that we are agents for.
2. Conform to all of the terms of the lease. Make sure you pay your rent on time. No pets if specified, and no disturbances that would cause complaints from your neighbors.
3. Notify property manager 60 to 90 days prior to the end of your lease in writing of you desire to pursue purchasing a home.
4. This rent credit is good on the resident's next real estate purchase at any point in time in the future.
5. The resident will receive the rent credit check at the time of the closing.
6. The rent credit applies only when the resident utilizes the Real Estate services and / or referral network of _____ _____ for his / her purchase.

_____ _____ _____ _____
Agent or   Date   Applicant   Date

CHAPTER 10

Contractors

When you pay contractors ahead of time, any personal problems that arise in their lives now become your problems. They will take any money you give them and forget about the material to buy for your job and put it towards solving their problem. It is not that they are intentionally planning to rip you off; although some are. I believe most start out with good intentions. They start out committing a small wrong, thinking they will make it better later. However, one small wrong added to another, then another, and then it escalates. Before they know it, they are too deep, and you are paying for it. Now your job gets done shoddily, half way, or not at all.

One day I stopped by a property where I had just hired a contractor to install shingles on the roof. He was on about the fifth row. It was obvious to me that he did not know what he was doing. Having worked as a shingler for a roofing contractor when I was sixteen years old. The shingles were being laid inappropriately. There was no way I was going to keep him working on anything!

I once had a contractor who was doing quite a bit of work for me. He took a $2,000 deposit on a garage that never was built. He kept stringing me on. Then he took off without paying his workers even though I had paid him for the work. I have had contractors perform poor workmanship, steal materials, steal a furnace, abandon jobs, and more. My goal is to help you avoid these problems.

Types of contractors

There are four (4) types of contractors.

- **Rip-off artist**
- **Jack-of-all-trades**
- **General contractors and sub-contractors**
- **The handyman.**

1. **Rip-off artists** - These are con-men. Their objective in life is to take as much money from people as they can while providing as little as possible in return. They generally hire workers from day-labor places who are drug addicts, alcoholics, lazy undependable people who just can not hold a job, etc.

2. **Jack-of-all-trades** - These generally start out to be well-meaning. However, they often have no real expertise, give poor workmanship, know a little about this or a little about that, and wing it when they do not know. Their workers are less competent than they are.

If you do not strictly follow the guide lines as stated herein, you will lose money. The above two types of contractors make up the majority, not the minority. You will meet these guys! Follow the guide lines strictly, and you will also eliminate them.

3. **General contractors and sub-contractors** - A general contractor is competent in all the trades. He may be expert in one or two areas and then supervise sub-contractors as they perform their specialty, for example hanging drywall, installing ceramic tile, electrical, plumbing, and heating systems. Where the general contractor is not expert in a specific trade he hires a sub-contractor who is, or he simply wants to divide up the work, to complete the job in a timely manner. These people are not infallible. However, they provide good workmanship, are honest in their dealings, and work with you to resolve problems when they arise.

4. **The handyman** - Generally they are not licensed or insured, but they are competent and honest in their dealings. They will admit when they do not know how to do something. Although they are generally not capable of handling large jobs, they are good for small jobs and miscellaneous repairs. They are great to have available for spur-of-the- moment repairs.

Of course, you will come across contractors who can be a mixture of any of the above. You would be very wise indeed to check your contractor out very carefully. Follow up on the progress of the work, and literally stay on top of them. Once you have a contractor who has proven himself to be trustworthy and capable, he will be a valuable resource for you.

Locating Contractors

You can locate contractors through several means. The least desirable sources are yellow pages, newspaper ads, and solicitors who come via the telephone and door-to-door. There are also the inspectors who offer a "free" inspection of your furnace or attic insulation, a termite inspection, or some other item. Of course, they find something wrong and offer to fix it at a hefty price. Surveys in several states indicate that, "homeowners who hired contractors based on radio, television or print ads, the yellow pages...have more problems with their home improvements."

Other advice I have heard is not to do business with family members or friends because more often than not hard feelings are the result. You be the judge of your own circumstances.

Best Sources to Pursue

- Referrals from friends and relatives. Of course, the referral should not be their friend or relative.
- People in your area who are having jobs done. Contractors usually hang their signs outside homes where they are working.
- Chamber of Commerce.
- Realtors or anyone else who has direct experience with the work of a contractor.
- Building material supply stores. These stores usually have a contractor's board with their business cards. The clerks usually know who the regulars are and who has a good reputation.
  Regardless of the source you use, get three to five bids and check them out strictly.

Questions to Ask a Contractor

When you question contractors, take notes on each one you talk to. The information will all run together later if you do not. Here is some information that you will want to consider learning as you conduct your questioning:

- How long has your company been in business? If a contractor has been in business three or more years and has a local address, these certainly are positive facts.
- How many crews does the contractor employ, and how many workers are there per crew? A one crew contractor is not a bad sign. It is just information to know.
- Can the contractor provide you three to six references of jobs he has recently completed? Also, can he provide references for the jobs he is currently working on?
- Will the contractor be using any sub-contractors? You will want the names and numbers of any sub-contractors before they start any work. You will also want to verify that they are paid!

The Reality of Real Estate Investing

- Will the contractor allow you to pull a credit report on them? How well they pay their bills is an indication of their business practices.
- Take note of the vehicle the contractor drives. Is it a junker, or is it professional looking?
- Drive by the contractor's home and business addresses. I do not feel that running a business out of his home is a negative. However, the appearance and how well-kept it is are serious factors. It is an indication of their pride of workmanship.
- Check out the contractor's credentials. If he is truly a contractor and not just a handyman posing as a contractor, expect him to produce a license. He should also have a certificate of insurance — liability and workman's compensation. Get a copy of each for your records. Verify with the Department of Licenses in your state that the license is current and in good standing. Do the same with the insurance company. **Red Flag!!** Be wary of anyone who tries to side-step or smooth talk his way past these items and wants you to just focus on his low price. Again, if it sounds too good to be true, you are right! Trust your first instinct. I learned the hard way. You bought this book so you could learn from my mistakes. Follow my advice, and you will save money and frustration.
- Get the references and actually call them!

    – Ask about the quality of the contractor's work.
    – Was he on time with the work?
    – Did they feel they got what they paid for?

- Check with City Hall, and the local consumer affairs department.
- Check with the Better Business Bureau.

Understand that these agencies cannot tell you if a contractor is good or bad. However, they can tell you if any complaints have been filed and if they have been resolved or are un-resolved. Also, keep in mind that bad contractors can operate under one name today and another one tomorrow. What was formerly known as "Joe Blow Super Duper Remodelers" with a long list of complaints on file today, tomorrow can be "Mother Theresa Remodeling Experts, Inc." with a squeaky clean record.

If a contractor has one or two complaints, ask about them. Investors / home-owners can be mean-spirited or rip-off artists themselves. Your final decision will not be based on this fact alone. You will consider all the facts.

If the opportunity exists, actually go and take a look at some of the contractor's work, or even go to a job he is currently working on.

Allen Watkins

Inspecting the Contractor's Work

Some things to look for:

♦ With vinyl and ceramic floor tile, are there gaps between the tiles? Are the tiles straight? Is the grout between the ceramic tiles sealed?
♦ If copper plumbing was installed and if a connection was made of copper to galvanized pipe, was a die-electric union used for the connection? If not, then over a couple of years a chemical breakdown takes place, and a leak occurs. This is one of many possible shortcuts a poor-quality contractor might use because the die-electric union costs more money and takes longer to install.
♦ Drywall: Observe how or ask the contractor what his procedure is for installing drywall. The concern is nails backing out in a few months or a year, creating unsightly walls and producing a hassle and expense to repair. The best installation procedure is to place liquid nail (contractor grade glue) on the 2 x 4's and then to use drywall screws to anchor it to the wall or ceiling.
♦ The above procedure would also apply to laying plywood floors or underlayment, using ring shank nails or screws.
♦ Roof: It is easy to see if the tabs are aligned straight from the ground. You should also check if the rows are straight from a side view and are not wavy like a snake. Check the tabs for four nails per shingle, not two. Aluminum flashing should be used in the valleys, next to walls, around pipes, and around chimneys. A rain drip guard should be installed on the edge of the roof before the first starter row.
♦ Greenboard: This is water-resistant drywall. It is most commonly used in bathrooms around the tub and shower areas. If you see someone using regular drywall in these areas, eliminate them! They are cutting corners because greenboard is more expensive, or they simply do not know what they are doing.
♦ Cleanliness of the job site: Some clutter and dirt is to be expected. After all there is construction work taking place. However, expect that the site should be picked up on a regular basis and especially at the end of the day.

These are just some tips to get you started. You will learn much more as you become involved. There is nothing like the experience of actually having to pay for contracting work. You will only know what I mean once you have done it.

When you are swaying back and forth between two different contractors, it is time to employ the Benjamin Franklin Decision Maker. List all the positives in one column and all the negatives in another about each contractor. This helps you get your thoughts and the facts organized. You can see all the facts before you at one time, and you are better able to make a decision. Do this separately on both contractors. Then compare and make your decision.

The Contractor Agreement

Get it in writing!

Prior to having a contractor come look at a job, make an itemized list of the work you want to be performed. Keep in mind you are going to get three to five different bids. Most contractors will assume you are getting more than one bid. Do not volunteer information, and do not lie if they do ask.

You will be surprised at the wide range of bids that come in. When I got bids for remodeling a 76-unit building, the high bid was $13,000 per unit, and the low bid was $3,500. There were several in the middle ranges. I went with one for $7,200.

If you leave it up to them to write up their own itemization, each bid is going to look different, making it hard to compare them. You need to prepare an itemized list and it should look similar to the following:

Itemized Bid

1234 Your Street, City, State

Exterior:

1. Roof — Tear off old shingles; install new quality grade felt paper and fiberglass shingles; install flashing complete with rain-guard. Install temperature controlled attic vent. _____

2. Scrape and paint all wood surfaces where peeling paint exists. Use quality grade primer where bare wood exists and a white color quality grade exterior flat latex paint. _____
3. Garage — Replace service door with quality exterior solid core. _____
4. Landscape — Mow and edge yard; trim bushes. _____

                     Total Exterior: _____

Interior:

1. Patch, prep, and paint walls and ceilings and currently painted wood trim throughout using quality grade primer over patched areas. Off-white

quality grade satin finish on walls and ceiling, semi-gloss on wood trim, kitchen walls, and bathroom walls. _____

2. Kitchen — Replace counter, sink, faucet, drain, and all plumbing complete using quality grade materials. Install white ceramic back splash, including stove area. _____
   - Remove old and install new underlayment and vinyl floor and new metal edging. _____
   - Clean wood cabinets inside and out; re-wax. Install new handles. _____

3. Bath — Replace medicine cabinet with a 3-mirrored door oak cabinet; install new oak toilet seat, paper holder, and towel bar. _____

4. Detail clean ceramic tub area and reseal grout, re-caulk tub with quality silicone tub caulk. _____

5. Floors — Strip and re-wax all hard wood flooring. _____

Total Interior: _____

All work is to be done in a quality workmanship-like manner. The home shall be detailed cleaned. Minor repairs that would be expected to bring the home in ready move in condition not specified on this agreement shall be deemed included.

Other details:
_____
_____
_____
_____
_____

Start date: _____   Total Bid: _____
Completion date: _____   Penalty per day not completed: _____

_____   _____   _____   _____
Signature   Date   Signature   Date

That should be enough to give you a good idea of what I mean. In the beginning you are on your learning curve and establishing rapport and a trusting relationship with the contractor you have screened and decided to take a chance on. In the beginning, also, you may be looking to the contractor for his suggestions on what should or should not be done. You can learn from this process. However, take the advice with a grain of salt and compare it with the next contractor's suggestions. It is not his money he is spending. It is going to take a worthwhile investment of time on your part. Do not take short cuts! Do not blindly trust!

The lowest bid is not necessarily the best bid. The lowest bidder may not possess a good business aptitude, or he may use poor workmanship. Check him out and consider all the facts. The lowest bidder can cost you the most money!

Paying the Contractor

"Money up-front for materials, please!" The contractor will say. You reply, *"I would like to; however, I am really uncomfortable giving money to someone I do not even know. You see, someone I know got ripped off doing that once."* You are not lying; that someone is me. Then you could say, *"Tell you what — until you and I have some established history, I will meet you at the building supply store and pay for the materials directly. Fair enough?"* Of course it is fair enough. Consider this: If the contractor does not have the ability to establish a line of credit or a credit card to acquire materials, how credible can he be? If they will not agree to it, ask why. He probably will not give you a straight answer. Just tell him that you will have to discuss it with your financial partner and get back to him. That is right! You are also going to play the role of middleman with the contractor. It gets you off the hook when a contractor tries to put you on the spot. Do not let your ego get in the way here. Build your ego with your personal friends and banker. You will be much better off having done so. If you end up blowing off a contractor, oh well, you move on to the next one. At least you got his bid numbers for comparison usage.

Some contractors will not ask for a dime until the entire job is completed. They have financial strength and know they can place a lien on your property if you try any funny business. You will still need proof that suppliers and sub-contractors were paid.

Labor Money

You are going to agree to pay for one-third of the work when one-third of the work is done; one-third more when one-third more of the work is done; and the balance upon completion. That is what you put in writing. However, you are only going to pay out the amount on the itemized list for an item that is completely done and that you can check off your list. Of course, there should always be other items that are started but not completed. That way the contractor is always owed some more money and has incentive to keep right on working. Do not let them talk you into wavering from this position. You sympathize with their need for more money; however, your financial partner is very strict on this issue, and there is nothing you can do. Just tell them, *"Get the next one-third of the work done, and I'll get you the money as agreed."*

Useful Clauses

- A $25 penalty will be incurred by the contractor for each day beyond the completion date until the work is 100% completed. (When the contractor first gives you his completion date, you automatically extend it by one week for good measure, and to show that you are being more than reasonable. Since you really do not want him to be penalized, and for your partner's knowledge, you will make the completion date one week later.)
- Any additions are to be approved ahead of time in writing and made a part of the contract.
- Should no one show up for work for three consecutive days and the contractor has not called to offer an explanation and progress report, the job will be considered abandoned. All money due per the agreement will be forfeited due to incomplete work. Another contractor will be hired to complete the job.
- There will be no alcoholic beverages or any drug use on the job site. If abuse is found to exist, there will be a forfeiture of the contract and any outstanding compensation. (That is a bold statement. You may not necessarily enforce it if a worker is found in violation without the contractor's knowledge. If the contractor deals with it appropriately, that is the determining factor.)
- Contractor is 100% responsible for all the materials on the job site, for any mistakes made by any workers or sub-contractors, and for the cost to replace any materials or correct any mistakes.
- The job site will be kept clean and neat at all times.
- Names and phone numbers of any sub contractors will be provided to the owner prior to their doing any work on the job site.
- Prior to the final payment the contractor will provide the owner with an appropriate lien waiver for materials and labor. (This is what a title company or mortgage company will want if they know work was done in order to place financing on your property, even though you may have other proof that the contractor is paid in full. This applies for a refinance or sell.)

You will also want proof that the contractor has paid the suppliers of the materials and the sub-contractors. Otherwise, you could end up paying for them again. If you do not pay your contractor, he can place a lien on your property until you do pay. If the contractor does not pay his suppliers or sub-contractors, they can also put a lien on your property until you pay them.

Obtain Knowledge

When you need to have work done and you know nothing about how it is done or what materials should be used, become informed! Do some research. You will be better prepared to know when a contractor is lying to you or when work is performed incorrectly. Knowledge of a contractor's work can ensure that you get full benefits of manufacturer warranties and guarantees of products and materials. For instance, some contractors will install asphalt roofing their own way for speed. However, if they do not install it the way the manufacturer details, the warranty may be voided. If something goes wrong with the roof, you, rather than the manufacturer, are responsible. This also applies to many other products and materials as well. There are also differences in quality of similar materials and between different name brands. Ask questions. Become informed. Home improvement centers employ some very knowledgeable people of the trades. Libraries are a good resource with how-to books and videos, and of course the internet.

Do Not Relinquish Control

Once the job starts, do not think that you can do something else and show up on the target completion day and all will be well. It will not work that way. Problems or questions arise. If you are easily available or visiting the job site regularly, you have the opportunity to give your input. Also, when something is being done, you can see if it is what you anticipated. If it is not, then you have the ability to make a change.

By being around, you reduce the possibility of your being ripped off. By this I mean that you can prevent the contractor from taking short cuts and not giving the quality you contracted for. Some examples:

Concrete driveway — You contracted for four inches. If you do not see it being poured and just see the finished product, you do not know if you got four or three inches. The same applies to an asphalt driveway.

Wall insulation — It is a tedious job to pump insulation between each and every 2 x 4. Did all of the walls actually get done and filled to the top? You cannot see inside the wall once it is done.

Paint job — Did they actually put on two coats or just one? You cannot always tell once the job is done.

Windows — Was insulation actually put in around the windows before the trim was put up?

Allen Watkins

There are many other possibilities. Now, this does not mean you have to be on the job site every minute. If you have screened the contractor properly, you probably have nothing to worry about. However, you do not let the contractor think that you trust him completely and have given full control of the job over to him. You have to keep him on his toes! Keep him honest! Show up at the job site unexpectedly. Do not allow your arrival to be obvious. Walk around observing what is going on. Say hello to the workers, and ask questions about what they are doing. Give words of encouragement and praise. Tactfully and politely let them know that you know the right way of how things should be done and you appreciate their efforts and pride of workmanship. If you do not know about something, ask, this is also an opportunity to learn. People like sharing their knowledge with others.

Try not to give a specific time when you will be visiting the job site. If you are asked what time you will be there and you say 9:00, show up at 8:00 or 8:30. Always keep them guessing. In this way you always maintain more control.

CHAPTER 11

Remodeling and Maintenance

The majority of homes you buy below market will need work. Some just need a little, some a great amount. I am happy to report that I have acquired an occasional "cream puff" that required no work. Sometimes the home already had a tenant in place and paying rent!

There are probably as many different ideas of how to remodel as there are people to do it. I will share with you some of my thoughts and opinions, and you can do with it what you will. However, I know if I had detailed instructions as contained herein when I first started, I could have avoided many mistakes.

The bottom line is the cleaner and neater your property is, the higher the desirability that attracts a qualified tenant or buyer, and the higher the rent or price it will demand. The better the quality of the materials used, the better durability and longer usage you will have.

The quality of the area and the people affect the extent and type of work you will want to do to any given property. To patch and repair, or to rip out and replace, that is the question. It is difficult to give you hard and fast rules; in fact, I cannot. However, I am going to attempt to give you what I will refer to as flexible guidelines.

The objective with any work you do to a property is, of course, to get more value out of it than what it cost you. A $2 return for every $1 of cost, is a good objective.

In my comments below I am attempting to describe in general terms some economic levels as it relates to the investment value of remodeling a home. With that said, let us consider lower, middle, and upper valued homes. First, there are some common denominators for all three.

- Everything should be clean and neat — sparkling!
- Always use neutral colors. Off-white is good for all the walls and ceilings. Light earth tones (beige) can be used for trim, etc.
- No wall paper! There are almost as many colors and patterns as there are people. It makes no sense to spend money on wall paper just to get tenants or buyers who do not agree with your choice of pattern or color and then want to change it. Just prep and paint.
- Old or bold-color carpets are out. Use light, neutral colors for all flooring. No dark colors anywhere! Dark colors make spaces seem smaller, and they have a negative effect on one's attitude and mood.

Light colors make a space appear larger, are bright and cheery, and have a positive effect on one's attitude and mood.

Lower Priced Homes
$60,000 and Below

Money is green everywhere, even in the rough neighborhoods. I have made some good money in these areas! See Case in Point # 16, 96th Pl. However, you must be careful. I have also had my fair share of vandalism and tenants dealing drugs. These kinds of areas are not for everyone. Of course, not all lower priced areas are rough. You just need to be on the lookout for bad elements that seem to exist more often in lower priced areas. Look around; talk to people in the neighborhood about the area. Talk to the postal carriers and to the neighbors of your subject home. Then make your best judgment.

Patching versus Replacing

In lower priced homes it just does not pay to do it up first class. You will not get all of your cost back if you replace everything with brand new items in a for-sale home, and things will get beat up in a rental. These are properties where you are going to patch and repair anything that is saveable. However, if the cost to patch or repair is one-half or more of the cost to replace with new, replace it with a new item. Of course, you will replace with a low-end new item that is durable. I will try to give you some specific examples.

- ♦ Windows — Wood, double-hung; follow the one-half or more rule. Keep in mind that storm windows with screens are required. If you decide to get new windows, they should be thermopane with screens. One way to approach this, of course, is to call some window installation companies. You will pay a high price, but with a reputable company you will get a good warranty.

I cannot resist telling you about an experience I had with one company. I was rehabbing a 76-unit building. The window company bid was $200,000 to replace all the windows and the front and rear doors. Through negotiation and our walking away from doing business with the company, they finally came back with their very best bid of $98,000 for the same work and materials. A considerable difference!!

If you can hook up with a window installer who does work on the side, that is how to get your very best price. He can buy from the manufacturers the same as the window companies. You can have the contractor / carpenter you normally work with do the job. He should be considerably cheaper than the window company as well. (The same considerations apply for new siding.)

In sprucing up existing windows, the items to consider are:

— replacing the old, cracked, and loose glazing.
— sanding, staining, and using polyurathane; or
— painting beige, white, or off-white semi-gloss paint.
— installing new locks and handles.
— replacing torn and tattered screens.
— cleaning all the glass.

- Kitchen Cabinets / Vanities — When made of wood, cabinets can be cleaned up and painted or refinished (sanded, stained, and polyurathaned) to look nice. Depending on the condition, even metal cabinets can sometimes be saved. Handles and counter tops need to be in good condition or replaced with new. Old, scratched up porcelain sinks should be replaced with double-bowl stainless steel.
- Hardwood floors — If they are in decent condition, stripping and re-waxing would be worthwhile. However, if they are in poor condition, sanding and refinishing is best.

Carpeting is not a good use of your money if you plan to rent. In certain areas when refinishing hardwood floors is cost-prohibitive, paint with a quality gloss deck paint. (A milk chocolate brown color has worked well for me.) You just clean the floor, and then roll on the deck paint. It makes a nice, clean finish, and it is durable and very economical. Better yet, once the tenant moves, it is easy and economical to do it again. Tenants use throw rugs. It works well at this value level. Refinishing the floor or putting in carpet is much more expensive to re-do after each tenant. When painting exterior steps, be sure to mix in sand which is available at most paint supply stores. This grit makes for a non-skid surface and is simply much safer.

Of course, if you have other than hardwood floors, you have no choice but to install carpet. I favor using Berber carpeting because it looks and wears great! If you look hard, you can find it at an economical price. Another avenue to consider for carpet is a wholesaler - re-seller. This is a person who removes quality carpeting from hotels that is still in good shape and then resells it to the public at a fraction of the cost. He gets paid to remove it and is paid a little on the resale. He is able to pass considerable savings on to the purchaser.

- Marlite paneling works well in bath rooms and for the back splash in kitchens.

- Aluminum Siding — When it is faded or just the wrong color, a fresh paint job can make it look like new. Of course, it must be prepared properly and the right kind of paint used. It is best applied with a paint sprayer which can be rented at your local rental center. Get advice from your nearest paint center. The same applies to slate siding. When there is a need to install new siding, I prefer vinyl. Installation is easier. It does not fade, dent, or become chalky, and repairs are easy.
- Evaluate the space you have to work with for an additional bedroom or two. Attic or basement spaces that can be finished increase both the selling value and the rental value.
- Kitchen and Bathroom Floors — A nice looking industrial tile works great because of its great durability when renting. When selling, look at vinyl tile with patterns. Choose neutral, light colors.

Middle Priced Homes
$60,000 to $100,000

Some of the items for lower priced homes also can work with middle priced homes. It is really a personal judgment call based on what you have to deal with on a case by case basis.

- Painting of floors is not acceptable. Sanding and refinishing hardwood floors is very worthwhile. They are beautiful; most people like them; they are easily maintained; and tenants can put down their own throw rugs.
- When carpeting, I still like to use Berber. I have never met anyone who did not like it. Of course, using a good quality pad makes a difference. Do not skimp!
- Marlite paneling is not the best use in this price range. It is best to go with ceramic tile for back splashes and around tubs. Some quality tub enclosure kits look nice, also.
- Ceramic tile for the floors is nice; however, you can also use quality vinyl tile or linoleum.

Upper Priced Homes
$100,000 and Up

These are better suited for fixing up and selling than renting. If you have a tenant go bad on you, the risk is substantially higher because the lost dollars add up much quicker. It is better to spread the risk around and maintain a higher cash flow. For example, instead of renting a $200,000 home, you could have rented four $50,000 homes. When you have an opportunity to get a good deal on an upper priced home, consider selling right away for a profit. Now you can take that profit and acquire more lower and middle priced homes. Of course, having $200,000 invested in a 6-unit apartment building with six incomes is a good consideration.

In reference to the remodeling of upper priced homes, no patching is allowed, while repairing depends on what it is. You want to do them up first class. They will sell quicker and for a better price.

My best advice (and this advice also works for lower and middle priced homes) in helping you gain knowledge and insight into your specific market is to schedule appointments through your local Realtor to view homes that are presently on the market in the area. This serves two purposes:

1. It gives you ideas about quality, conditions, and amenities that your competition has to offer, as well as remodeling ideas.
2. It also helps you to better understand what a competitive price for your home will be.

Keep in mind 99% of buyers do not look at just one home and buy it. They look at several in an area that match their desires. Therefore, remodel and price your home to be competitive. Of course, you should factor in homes that have sold and closed in the neighborhood, also. Although you cannot do an interior inspection on the sold homes, do a drive-by and read the Realtor's comments on the Multiple Listing Service computer printout. You will get ideas about what to do to make your home competitive.

Of course, all this takes time. Any worthwhile endeavor or educational pursuit takes time. Once the time is invested, it will bring you unlimited amounts of return. Take short cuts or try to fly by the seat of your pants, and you will be caught short. It will cost you much more in time, money, and stress.

As my dad and mom told me as a kid growing up, *"If it is worth doing, it is worth doing right the first time."* Oh, how much farther along I would be if I had put this to the test more often instead of taking short cuts and proving it right.

General Tips

- Roof shingles should get four nails per shingle, not two or three. For a new roof, one inch nails are OK; for a re-roof, one and a half inch; for a third roof, one and three quarters inch. Most codes require that prior roofs be torn off before a fourth one is installed.

- When putting up drywall, make sure the contractor glues and screws the drywall. This makes for a more solid wall, and you do not have the problem of nails backing out. Ring shank nails may be OK to use however, screws are better.
- For new plywood floors, they should be three quarter inch tongue and groove, glued, and screwed. This reduces squeaky floors.
- When replacing a section of copper plumbing and the water shut-off still allows a trickle of water which does not allow the pipe to get hot enough to complete the solder, take a slice of bread and "mush" it into a ball. Stuff it down the pipe. it will stop the trickle long enough to complete the solder, and then it will break down and allow water to flow.
- For underlayment, use proper underlayment nails which are designed to prevent backing out and are nailed six inches apart.
- When creating additional rooms, as in an attic space, some contractors might try using 2 x 3's instead of 2 x 4's for building the walls. The 2 x 3's are not strong enough, and can lead to other problems.
- Some contractors will try to use three / eights inch drywall instead of half inch. It is too flimsy! There is very little price difference, but half inch weighs more.
- When considering to improve a basement, check into what measures have already been taken to prevent flooding or water leaks from the basement wall. Determine if there is some existing risk. Look for signs of past water damage such as stained, mildewed, or water lines along baseboards or walls, cracks in the basement walls, rust around the bottom edge of the furnace or hot water heater.
- When finishing a basement, do not secure paneling or drywall to furring strips. Instead use 2 x 4's. The masonry nails can chip the walls, and the paneling or drywall will not be as true or level as with 2 x 4's.
- When pouring concrete for a garage slab or for a sidewalk, it should be at least four inches thick with a four inch base of sand or gravel. It should be finished by a mason so that it is nonskid, rather than slick.
- To get rid of fleas it is not necessary to pay for an exterminator and deal with the mess or chemicals. Simply take a small lamp and place it on the floor in the middle of the room. Then take a pie tin or plate, fill it with water mixed with dish washing liquid. Your result will be many dead fleas in the water.
- For roach problems I recommend a roach paste formula on the hot links page of my web site. www.HomeBargains.com

Maintenance

Maintenance is a necessary part of life for any homeowner or landlord if that person is wise about preventing future problems and additional expense. If you are a do-it-your-self person, that is good at least initially, in my opinion. I have learned through personal experience that there is nothing like understanding what it takes to do a job until you have done it yourself. Then delegation is a factor in your continued growth and success.

This is where a handyman can really be useful. He can free up your time, which is certainly more valuable utilizing your ability to make deals than getting your hands dirty. Doing the work yourself is like losing a dime to save a nickel! Or equally essential to your success, having someone else do the work gives you more time to devote to your family. Balance in life is a necessary element of success. I do not believe a workaholic actually accomplishes more. He just simply works less smart and longer to accomplish the same amount. I speak from personal experience.

Routine Maintenance

You should put routine maintenance into your lease rider for your tenant of single family dwellings to perform. Of course, you cannot depend 100% on that happening. Some tenants just simply lack the ability and others will be just lazy. Therefore, you will need your handyman to go by and check if it is happening and, if not, do it. When warranted you may even charge the tenant for the service call. Items that would be included in routine maintenance:

- Furnace filters should be changed every thirty days. The cost is only about fifty cents each. Even when you explain to the tenant how this creates much healthier air for their family to breath, some still do not do it. It also lessens the strain on and extends the life of your furnace motor.
- Gutters need the leaves cleaned out each year after they are done falling. If leaves are allowed to remain in the gutters, they plug up the down spouts and water backs up and can overflow the gutter. This will cause rot to the fascia board and can continue on into the house. This also creates additional weight in the gutter. When it freezes and icicles form, even more weight pulls slowly on the gutter supports. Over time these supports become loose, sag, and start to rust out.
- Ensure gutter downspout extensions are working adequately to take water away from the foundation.

Allen Watkins

- Make sure drains have screen covers so that the accumulation of hair and other small items do not cause clogged drains and a back up.
- The drain hose to the washer should have a screen sack over it, also. This inexpensive minor effort prevents expensive rod out jobs. To improvise, a woman's panty hose will serve the purpose.
- For tree roots in the sewer lines, have the tenant flush a pound of lime powder down the toilet every couple of months. As the lime is slowly washed through the lines, tree roots retract from it.
- Door stops should be checked. They need to be on each door to prevent the need of repairing holes in the walls.
- Check all the faucets and toilet bowls for dripping water. This is pennies down the drain, and pennies do add up.

If you feel saving pennies is too minor to consider, I will make you the following deal. I will pay you $10,000 on the first day of our agreement. In exchange you will sign a recordable note secured against what- ever you have of value, with the following "you owe me" terms. On the first day of our agreement you will owe me one cent, the second day two cents, the third day four cents, the fourth day eighth cents. The amount will continue to double like this each day for a total of thirty days. That total amount is what will be due me. Do not delay, let's make this deal; call me now!

CHAPTER 12

Contracts and Clauses

I cannot possibly cover everything there is to know about contracts in this chapter, nor shall I attempt to do so. It is always suggested that you seek the advice of your attorney regarding any contractual agreement you enter into.

I do not recommend that you need to talk with your attorney first, before entering into a contract. Sometimes delaying to tie up a property in writing can cost you a deal. By being prepared to act immediately, based on the surface information you have available, you can be the early bird that gets the worm. The best deal I ever did was because I acted and did not hesitate to tie up a property. See Cases in Point # 5, Barry & # 25, Crete.

By doing this, it does not mean you are taking a chance at losing a great amount of money or buying something you do not want. It means you are maximizing your opportunities to make money.

Attorney's Right to Review

Depending on the circumstances when you are putting a deal in writing, if you feel the need to protect yourself, do so by inserting a little clause known as the "Attorney's right to review." A sales contract with this clause says:

"Subject to a review by the attorneys of the buyer and seller within three business days after the signing of this contract."

You would use this in the case of your not being sure about the circumstances while wanting to tie the property up immediately. This acts as your out clause. Of course, it works for the seller the same as it works for you.

It is important to realize that you want the seller's attorney to approve the contract, or at least it should be obvious to anyone who might look at the situation in the future that you provided the seller the opportunity to seek an attorney's advice. There is one very important reason for this. Although you make a very good deal for yourself with someone in a very motivated position and even close the purchase, it does not stop that person from changing his mind later and thinking that you took unfair advantage of him in a desperate situation. Of course, the objective is to never take advantage of anyone. You only want to help someone out of a bad situation and have it be worthwhile for you to extend yourself. However, how someone else may view the situation looking in from the outside is the important element — for instance, a Judge. What if the seller were to hire an attorney after the fact and file a lawsuit. Could his attorney present a case before a Judge that you took advantage of him acting under duress? Could a Judge rescind your contract and have you compensate the seller for his trouble with you? The fact of the matter, as I understand it, is that a Judge can do what his conscience tells him within the confines of the law. It may seem to him that you are a person who appears to know what you are doing and the homeowner or property owner appears to be naive and under duress.

I hope I have driven this point home hard enough for you. I have personally never experienced the above problem because I have always seen to it that the sellers have their attorney's approval, or at least that I provided them the opportunity and encouraged it. Whether or not they actually do it, of course, is up to them. Keep in mind they have to pay for that attorney. I have even offered to pay the attorney fee as part of the transaction, but sometimes it is like the saying, *"You can lead a horse to the water, but you can not make him drink!"*

The "Attorney's Right to Review" clause is the insurance to protect you in the event you should ever have to appear before a Judge. Actually it would be foolish for the same attorney to file such a lawsuit after the fact, since he approved it to start with, and another attorney's case would be more against the first attorney who approved the deal than with you.

Now in my caution to insure that sellers get legal advice and approval from an attorney of their choosing, you may be wondering if I ever lost a deal because of the attorney? Yes, I have. Do I think they may have done a deal themselves or with someone they know? Yes, I do. It happens. However, I would rather lose a deal that way than have the alternative and have it cost me money. Another thing to remember, I would not advise recommending an attorney to the sellers. Keep your distance. Have them get a referral from one of their friends or relatives.

The "Attorney's right to review" clause would have no use when you are having the seller deed the property over to you right then and there with the closest notary as in my above Cases in Point. It is because, based on the facts you have before you, your knowledge, and your experience, you have decided you need to act now before someone else does. By having someone deed over his property to you, does not automatically make you liable for the liens against it. It just gives you the controlling position. If you discover there are encumbrances you did not count on, then you are free to walk away from it. Just because someone deeds his property over to you does not mean you have to record it.

An owner can deed his property over to someone via a Quick Claim Deed, which means with any liens that may be against it, there is no warranty of clean title. Or, via a Warranty Deed, which means the only liens if any, are being disclosed to you.

There are some general things I could cover here, but I will not because it would just be for filling up pages, and that is not what this book is for. Certain things will be covered in any general contract you pick up at an office supply store or from a realtor or attorney. Your attorney will also insure that you are getting clear title, the proration of taxes, etc. It is my intention to cover things that are not generally covered.

Minimum Essential Terms

"*Statute of Frauds*" is the law that requires contracts for the sale of real estate to be in writing so that they may be enforceable.

I want to mention the minimum, essential terms needed to make an enforceable contract for the purchase of real estate. They are:

1. A description of the land sufficient to identify it. The common address is adequate for the contract. The legal description will be confirmed with the title report through your attorney.
2. The price.
3. The terms of sale, if not cash (earnest money, financing, closing date).
4. Signatures.

Home Inspection Clause

The Home Inspection Clause is standard in most realtor contracts. If it is not in the contract you pick up from the office supply store, you will certainly want to add it.

"Buyer shall have the right to have a home inspection performed at buyer's expense within ___ (Generally 5) days from acceptance. Should this inspection reveal repairs that the buyer has not already accepted, then the buyer shall have the right to re-negotiate the contract. If an agreement between buyer and seller can not be accomplished, buyer shall receive a refund of his earnest money deposit. The following repairs are accepted by the buyer with this contract. _____."

The purpose of this clause is so a buyer will comfortably make an offer on a property before having to expend money for a detailed inspection.

Other Clauses

There are probably hundreds of clauses you could use to cover yourself in a contract. However, to attempt to use them all or too many clauses will insure that you do not have a contract to start with. The goal is to cover yourself completely and keep it simple. Below are some clauses to consider when appropriate:

- State that you are buying the property as an investment, and it is your immediate desire to make a profit.
- Purchaser has right to show the property prior to closing.
- The sooner you line up a tenant or buyer the better for you, of course. See Case in Point # 17, Bruce-Harvey. However, you may be walking on eggshells. Do not do it if the seller is uncomfortable. It could cost you the deal.
- Owner shall give purchaser possession upon closing, or closing will be postponed.

Understand that the seller has developed a very bad habit of living mortgage and rent free. Some people have a hard time breaking bad habits. If you close and allow them to remain in possession, you are asking for trouble for a number of reasons.

1. Now the pressure is off. They did not keep their word to the bank; do not fool yourself into believing they will treat you any different.
2. Their friend or relative starts to talk with them. He convinces them that your deal was a bad one, regardless of how good it actually was.
3. The friends or relatives they were going to move in with have changed their minds.
4. Suddenly the apartment they had lined up is not ready.
5. They cannot line up a rental truck.

On, and on, and on. These people will seem so nice and sincere, but if you give in, you will get burned. They will make you put pressure on them by filing an eviction, or they will ask for more money, and they may cause more damage to the home. **Be firm! No possession! No closing! No money!** Some people will require you to hold their hand and push them to prepare and do what they need to do to get on with their lives. See Case in Point # 12, Evergreen Park. You may need to help them find an apartment, get help moving or renting a truck, and so on. The deal better be worth it to go through all this hassle. Keep in mind that there is some spiritual reward in just helping a fellow human being. However, helping someone does not mean allowing yourself to be taken advantage of. Sometimes it may require you to put up their first month's rent or security deposit or both, or pay for the truck rental. Of course, never give them the money for this. You pay the landlord or truck rental agency directly.

- The condition of the property is to be maintained as when first viewed or better. A final-walk through will be performed just prior to the closing.

- The earnest money is to be held by the purchaser's attorney (or you could allow the seller's attorney to hold it; he is bound by law) and disbursed at closing. If a closing fails to take place at the agreed-upon date and time, the earnest money shall be immediately refunded to purchaser.
- This contract is contingent upon the purchaser having fourteen working days from receipt and approval of all leases, records, preliminary title report, underlying encumbrances, and being allowed a complete physical inspection of the property, to remove all contingencies in writing. Then and only then will the earnest money be deposited, or this contract is null and void, and the earnest money check shall be refunded.

Now the seller is under pressure to provide you with all the information necessary for you to evaluate the deal thoroughly, to verify information and to determine if it is still reasonable for you to go ahead and close on the purchase or re-negotiate the deal. More often than not when verifying information that has verbally been given, you will find it does not match what you were told. That is why this clause is so very important.

Earnest Money Clause

First and foremost, never give earnest money directly to a seller. Think about what that seller is going to do with that money. That is right, deposit it in their checking account. If the deal falls through you will have a much harder time getting it back, if at all. Every contract has a line naming the company to hold the earnest money. The seller's attorney, or even the buyer's attorney, could hold it. All of them are governed by law and limited to depositing it in a non-interest bearing account, and they can only withdraw it with the written direction of both buyer and seller. However, I say why let anyone deposit your money until you know for sure if you have a deal. After the blank where you fill in the amount of the earnest money, write the following:

"To be deposited only upon removal of contingencies."

Now, even though you have given them a check, it cannot be deposited until you have removed all the contingencies. If the deal falls through, you are entitled to get the money back any way. Therefore, why should any one hassle with depositing it in his escrow account until it is a sure thing?

Do not point out this clause to the agent or seller. Once you have the signed contract in hand, remind the agent or seller of the clause because you do not want the check accidently deposited anyway. Some realtors will try to tell you they have to deposit it within twenty four hours; that is the law. Respond by telling him it only applies when the seller and buyer have not agreed to it being deposited at a different time. Because of the earnest money clause, the law does not apply, and he is relieved of the legal obligation to deposit it within twenty four hours until the contingencies are removed. Do not allow yourself to be pressured into doing otherwise. With this clause you buy yourself time without spending money until you have enough information on the property to make a good decision.

I should admit while I have made deals with owners, the majority of my acquisitions have been from auctions. It is simply an easier process.

License Tip

If you have a real estate license, make that fact known up-front verbally. Say something like, *"Oh, by the way, Mr. Seller, for the record I just want you to know that I do have a real estate license. I am looking at your home to buy it myself, but I just want you to know that."* Then move on to something else, such as, *"Would you mind showing me through the property and pointing out any repairs you are aware of that need to be done."* When writing a contract, **next to your signature write "A licensed Realtor"** or as appropriate. Disclosing this fact is required by law.

Tax Tip

If you are bringing back payments current for a seller, do not structure the deal so that the payments are brought current as part of the purchase price. If the purchase price is $75,000 and the arrears are $3,000, it is as if you gave the seller the $3,000. He, of course, has to pay up the arrearage with it. A more advantageous way would be to make the purchase price $72,000, and you pay the $3,000 in arrearage at the closing. Now you have a $3,000 tax deduction. This method can work for other seller expenses as well.

CHAPTER 13

Marketing Strategies

Understand to do this subject justice would require a whole additional book. Infact, I have written that book. Entitled "Home Marketing Strategies" that can be found on my web site www.HomeBargains.com. Check it out, you'll find it much more enlightning than what I am able to include in this chapter especially when it comes to dealing with realtors. The information I provide will save you thousands of dollars.

I approach this subject from three different perspectives:

1. Home owner who has lived in and sold several homes.
2. Investor who is concerned about net profit.
3. Real Estate Broker who understands the value that Realtor's services can have for the cost of the commission.

As soon I have possession of a home I intend to sell, a For Sale sign goes up. The strategy is in the fact that even though the home may not be in tip top showing condition, my objective is to sell A.S.A.P. I know very well that the buyers who are in the market today will likely not be in the market next week because they have already bought. My philosophy is to give buyers a chance to be aware of my property. I have nothing to lose. Sometimes I have sold a property "As Is" for a reasonable profit and not had to deal with the fix up. Other times I have gotten a buyer with vision who wants me to finish the work. Meanwhile, they work on getting their financing in place to close on the purchase as soon as I am done with the work.

I do not recommend just letting a home sit there waiting for that buyer who can see past the "not up to par" appearance.

There are less of those type of buyers out there than those who want everything from the drive by curb view to the interior inspection.

Preparing to Sell

The most important reason that a home sells or does not sell is its "emotional appeal." Many buyers in today's market buy on emotion. They drive by, walk in,

Allen Watkins

and if the home hits them the right way, that's it; the home is sold. The following suggestions may help make your home more emotionally appealing:

1. First impressions last. The first view that a potential buyer gets is that of the front of the home. That impression is a lasting one. Infact, some people eliminate a home from consideration without ever going inside. Walk out to the street and look at your home as if you were the buyer. What things do you notice. Positive and negative, then set about to eliminate the negative and improve upon the positive. It is important to have the landscaping green and neatly trimmed. Having a lawn treatment company come out and service your lawn to give it that luscious full green look. The entry area, and front door are a focus point, make it as sharp as it can be. Freshly painted neat and clean! Flowers, plants as appropriate. I am sure some of the homes that I have sold is a result of my wife's efforts with decorating with flowers, plants, shutters on the windows etc. A little investment here can go a long way.

Also, the paint on the exterior of the home should be bright and crisp. The siding, window trim, soffitt, fascia, and gutters. A little touch-up of the home can make the difference between a quick or slow sale. It can also affect the final sales price.

2. Decorate for a quick sale. No faded or dirty walls or trim. Clean and paint with neutral colors. Ceilings painted white brighten up rooms. I personally love natural wood finishes, and think what a shame when I see nice wood trim painted. So do a lot of other people. Clean and give it a fresh coat of wax. Make your windows sparkle, replace torn screens, clean blinds and other window treatments. Spotted and dirty carpets, peeling wallpaper, etc., reduce appeal. Potential buyers do not want to guess how the home could look. Show them how sharp it can be. Make it sparkle with cleanliness!

3. Light attracts and darkness rejects. Let the sun shine in. Open drapes, blinds, and turn on lights. If you are accustomed to using low wattage bulbs, replace them with 100 or 75 watt bulbs. Let the buyer see how bright and cheerful your home is.

4. Repairs can make a big difference. Dripping faucets, loose knobs, sticking doors, stains, discolored caulk around the tub, and other minor flaws often suggest to the buyer that the home has not been properly maintained. Most buyers want to move right in and relax. Some are willing to take on repairs if they feel like they are getting a bargain.

5. Make your home look big. Too much furniture or clutter makes a home appear smaller. A neat well ordered home without excess furniture appears larger. Nobody wants to live in a crowd. Remove excess items and furniture from your rooms and closets. Make them neat and organized. Store things in your basement, attic, at a friends or relative, or rent a storage unit. However, not in the garage, it should be neat, clean, organized, and spacious as well. A buyers will perception of your neatly organized home with plenty of space, helps them visualize it as theirs. That is the first step toward the prospect becoming the new owner.

6. Kitchens and bathrooms often sell homes. Kitchens are still the center of a home and can make or break a deal. If the floor covering is worn, replace it with neutral light patterns. Carpet in the kitchen and baths is disliked by most people. Clear counter tops of small appliances and all miscellaneous items. You want to entice the buyer with as much work space as possible. Check and repair caulking, tile, faucets, etc. Sometimes replacing handles on cabinets makes them much more appealing. Make these rooms sparkle.

7. To many people, annoying pets, loud music, and bad odors can affect emotional appeal when a home is being shown. People take up space and can make a buyer feel uneasy. If your kids have friends over ask them to play in the back yard or take the dog for a walk. A barking dog is just a noisy unwanted distraction. Confine them in a kennel during a showing if no other options are available. Complete silence is not golden for prospective buyers. Pleasant soft music at a low volume sets a comfortable mood for buyers.

Please remember that everyone's senses are very active when they are making major life decisions, and spending their hard earned money. The aroma of fresh baked cookies, cake, bread, or pies certainly adds to the buyer's experience creating a desirable atmosphere.

8. When a Realtor is involved let them do their job. Every agent works differently. It is not necessary that the agent be a motor mouth when showing your home. The agent's most important job is to bring the potential buyer to your home. If it is emotional, it will sell. Too much talk can destroy a possible sale.

The same applies when not using a Realtor. Do not be a chatter box. When showing the rooms do not point out the obvious, like this is the living room. Instead, say something positive about each room, like the fire place has a gas starter, the tile floor in the bath is new, installed 1 month ago, etc

Please give the above some thought. Emotional appeal will result in a quicker sale at a higher price. One of the most difficult things for a seller to do is see his own home through a buyer's eyes.

Pricing Your Home

You can ask any price you want, take into consideration all the meaningful, valuable experiences of your family. The hard work you have put into it over the years, however, those emotional items only have value to you, not the buyer, or an appraiser. If you over price your home, it will simply just help sell other homes in the area. If you under price your home it will sell quickly yes, however, you will feel you have been cheated. By your own doing of course. Do not just pick a number out of the air or based on what a neighbor says they sold or paid for a their home. Your price should be based upon factual verifiable data.

The best method, and the same method used by Realtors and appraisers is comparing your home with other homes in your area that have sold.

Comparable Market Analysis (C.M.A.)

A comparable market analysis is performed by Realtors and is similar to what an appraiser does to determine the value of a property. It is free of charge, and Realtors will readily perform one for you in the hope of getting a listing. The M.L.S. is a valuable resource for obtaining information on similar homes in an area to compare amenities, make adjustments accordingly, and, based on the sold figures, arrive at what is deemed fair market value. The actives (your competition) are then taken into consideration, and the market list price is determined.

You can have three Realtors and three Appraisers do an analysis on your property and arrive at six different numbers. However, they would all likely be within close range of one another. Each individual's opinion and personal judgment plays a role in the process because it is not an exact science. I would advise that you have the agent explain and that you listen intently on how he arrived at his suggested list price. Have him show you the M.L.S. printouts and the information on them. Learn the process very well. If you have a good experienced agent. The opinion can be respected. The more you know and understand about the process, the more confident you will be of his price. You will also be better able to discern a new agent versus an experienced one, and you can differ in opinion should it be warranted.

While you do not have the ability to view the interior of homes that have sold, and neither do Realtors or Appraisers, I recommend that you have a Realtor show you homes in your area on the market for sale that would be your competition. Walk through using a buyer eye and take note of all the positives and negatives. This can be a real eye opener now when returning to look at your own home.

Now with a more accurate idea of the competitions amenities you can arrive at a more accurate price of your home after also considering the following data on the comparables.

- ♦ Location: proximity to busy streets, parks, rail road tracks, electrical power lines, commercial developments, etc.
- ♦ Size: Adjustments for differences in square footage is part of the equation to arrive at the average market price.

The Reality of Real Estate Investing

- Styles are generally just a consideration in the eye of the beholder. Although, it is generally felt that a 2 story has more value than a 1 story.
- Age: A very old home in good shape perhaps, but with no updating, would have less value than a new home or even one of the same age that has been updated.
- Construction: Brick having the most value, then aluminum or vinyl sided, then frame.
- Condition: Sharp and clean all the way around, or torn and tattered around the edges, mainly affects appeal and desirability. Which translates into value, in the eye of the beholder.
- Lot size, shape, and landscape. There are Better Homes and Gardens landscapes, and your bread and butter landscapes. Affects desirability and value.
- Original asking price VS actual selling price of the solds. Keep in mind generally speaking a buyer never anticipates paying full price. Unless your fortunate enough to be in an area of high demand and you priced your home right to start with, then full price is possible. Looking at what the original price VS the sold price of the comparables will answer for you if you should hold firm or expect to negotiate. Having the proper documentation to justify your price handy, to show the purchaser or Realtor making an offer, certainly gives you more ammunition to work with in your negotiation.
- Market time: How long were the comparables on the market before they sold. How much pressure you are under to sell quickly, certainly is a factor in pricing your home. If you want to sell a lot quicker than the average market time, then you will need to set your price slightly below the comparables. If your under no pressure and the average market time is within reason for you, then you can price your home at the average price of the comparables. If in your comparison with the other homes, your home is obviously superior, looking through the eyes of a prospective purchaser of course, and not the eyes of an emotional seller, then you may be justified in setting your home price a little above the comparables.
- Amenities. Whether there is a privacy fence, chain link, or none at all. Is there a deck, how large is the garage, is there central air, a fireplace, jacuzzi, etc.

Placing a value on all the differences and then adding or subtracting from the comparables sold price, helps you arrive at what is perceived a fair price for your home, compared to that specific home. Do that with at least 3 sold comparables and then average the price of the 3, or go with the adjusted price of the comparable that is most similar to your home.

Allen Watkins

There are charts available that estimate the value of different amenities to use as a guideline, Realtors use them. The charts are prepared by different entities. Below is a chart I acquired from a loan officer at a mortgage company.

Also, Realtors that you interview initially, will make their adjustments. You can ask them how they arrived at their recommended price, and have them show you specifically how they calculated the adjustments. What value they put on each of the amenities. Now, some of you will be concerned about wasting the Realtors time when you know you will be marketing yourself. Realize that if you do not sell in 2 to 3 months, you will likely list with a Realtor anyway. So these interviews are preliminary in the event you are unable to sell yourself. May the best Realtor win the chance to get your listing.

It is not an exact science to price a home as you can see, that would just make it too easy. One thing is certain, it is easier to come down in your price than it is to go up once on the market.

The major commercial advertisers in business seem to always set prices on their products by rounding down to the nearest nine. Since they spend millions of dollars, I tend to follow the same strategy. It makes sense to me. Which sounds better to you as a buyer, $90,000 or $89,900?

Marketing Activities

Whether you are marketing a property yourself or with a Realtor, there are some marketing activities that have less value than the M.L.S. However, they are activities that sometimes produce a buyer. You can do these yourself or pay a Realtor through the commission to do them. Any activity a Realtor agrees to do for you should be specifically detailed on the listing agreement. Of course, some people choose to just rely on the M.L.S.

"For Sale" Yard Sign

This is the lowest cost advertising you will do. Use a sign that is about 2'x3''' in size, with the same information on both sides. Place it where it is most visible in the ground near the curb and perpendicular to the road. This will allow it to be easily seen and read by people passing in either direction. It should be simple. For example:

Home
For Sale
708-922-3777
By Appointment Only

Safety Precautions

One of the disadvantages of marketing a property without a Realtor is that your opening your doors to complete strangers. Most people are just shopping for a home and are honest however, there is that small percentage of people who may have other motives. So caution should be exercised.

- Keep a log book of all your contacts. Names, phone numbers, and notes.
- By appointment only on the yard sign is an important safety precaution. If someone rings your bell anyway wanting to see your home, tell them that you have company so it is just not a good time, to please call the number on the sign. Say goodbye and close the door. It is not worth taking a chance letting complete strangers into your home without being prepared.
- You will get requests from people calling to do a drive by. Say "I'll be happy to give you the address. May I have your name please? Phone number? Is this your home number? Oh! I'm burning cookies in the oven! I'll call you back!" Hang up immediately! Now, you call the local name and address information number. (in the Chicago area it is 708-796-9600) punch in the number, then the computer tells you the name and address that belongs to that number. If it matches, so far so good. If not, you will need to question them further. Call them back apologize for having to hang up, and proceed with the conversation. Bottom line, never give out information to someone with whom you are not comfortable. Takes a little effort granted however, you and your family are worth protecting.
- When possible never show the home by yourself. Have a friend or relative just be present. They could be reading a book or the newspaper. When that is not possible arrange with a friend or relative to call 15 minutes after the showing starts. If they call while the prospective purchaser is still there, say loud enough to be heard that you will call back in a couple minutes once they leave. If you don't call they should call you again. Of course, the friend or relative will know you are taking a safety precaution, and that the police should be called immediately if you do not answer the phone.
- Items of value like jewelry, collectors' items, toys of value, etc., within easy reach should be put out of sight.

Creating a Brochure

While you are viewing other homes that are on the market for sell you will be picking up flyers or brochures that the sellers have prepared about their homes.

You will want to prepare something similar. Take the good ideas you see and improve upon the rest. It is basically an information sheet about your home. Provide all the details you would like to have if you were the purchaser. Remember also, the buyers are likely seeing other homes as well., you want them to easily be able to remember your home. You may want to include a color photo of your home. Once buyers have an interest in your home they will start to ask specific questions. You'll want to try to have them already answered on the brochure. Then you should have a file folder put together with all the documentation to back up your information. For example:

- the lot size, have a copy of the survey in your file.
- taxes, have a copy of the most recent tax bill.
- utilities, have a copy of the last 12 statements.
- warranties for appliances, heating, air conditioning, or anything else that may apply. Know first that it is transferable to the purchaser.
- a copy of any inspections that you may of had done. Keep in mind it is still reasonable for a buyer to acquire their own inspection report. Use yours to compare.

Advertising

Advertising is your second most valuable market exposure tool. (Next to the M.L.S.) Places to advertise:

- local newspapers, neighborhood and city
- homes magazines

There are by-owner and other magazines that only allow Realtor advertising. These are most plentiful. You could work out something creative with a Realtor. For example: you pay for the ad, the Realtor places it. Your phone number goes in the ad. You might allow the Realtor a quarter of the page to advertise another property with their number. Use whatever your creative thought waves come up with.

The purpose of advertising for Realtors is:

- Name exposure
- To generate buyer and seller leads

Yes, they would like to sell the home they are advertising. However, rarely does a buyer buy the home in the ad they originally called on. The Realtor may show the home to ad callers because it is certainly good for the seller to see them showing his home. After determining details of price range, areas interested in

The Reality of Real Estate Investing

and features desired, the Realtor will search the M.L.S. for other homes to show. Very rarely will a buyer look at only one home and buy it. Not only is it just not wise, the Realtor really has a duty to recommend they look at more than one. This is true especially in this day of Realtors also representing the interest of buyers.

Your purpose for advertising is to create inquires about your home. Which you will sift through to determine who are the prospective purchasers.

Writing Advertising

In describing your home, accentuate the positive! Do not mention the negatives or point them out and try to explain them. Do this only if they are asked about. Of course, this does not mean that you hide problems that should be properly disclosed. It is far better to deal with and even pay for correcting a problem than to face a lawsuit later.

- What was it about the home that attracted you to it?
- What improvements have you made?
- Always use the word home, not house. Home gives more of a personal feeling.
- If you have a home with only one bath, why pay to advertise that fact. People assume a home has at least one bath. The same is true with a one-car garage; just mention garage. Even if the buyer is looking for a two-car garage, once you are talking to them about the other features like the nice huge kitchen that the wife says she has to have when she sees it, the two car garage could be forgotten. Buyers often do not buy a home with exactly everything they wanted. It can be a give and take situation between the husband and wife. Some feature is usually compromised.
- The number of bedrooms is essential information.
- Your purpose for an ad should be to draw the greatest amount of interest for the least amount of money. Making an ad lengthy with detailed descriptions does not draw more interest; it just costs you more money, and this reduces the number of times you will be able to run an ad. A short ad with carefully chosen words of the home's highlights is best. Details can be answered once they are talking with you. Some buyers will overlook some negatives if the positives are really good for them.
- Always state the asking price. Studies have determined that many people simply do not respond to ads with no price.

- Include the name of your town or neighborhood. You are not trying to make the phone ring with a number of leads, as a Realtor would, you just want a buyer for your home.

Open Houses

Open houses are much like snag fishing. You throw in your line and hook, whip it around, and hope that you snag a fish.

With an open house, you open your home to anybody and everybody, hoping that a qualified buyer walks in and likes it. Personally, I feel it is one of the lowest productive activities. In all fairness, it does occasionally produce a buyer. If nothing else for marketing your home on a Saturday or Sunday afternoon is being done, well, some activity is better than none. Safety precautions mentioned earlier should be taken.

Tips for planning an Open House

- When using a Realtor or by yourself, so that you or your agent are not just sitting there doing nothing between showings, secure from the criss cross directory (formerly known as the Haines or Donnelly Directory) at your local library a list of all the people in your neighborhood. The directory is organized by streets, listing all the names and numbers. Call the people in the vicinity of your home and invite them to the open house. You never know, they might be renting and thinking of buying or may know of someone else who may be interested.
- Weekend afternoons are the best hours.
- Place an ad in the newspaper announcing the open house.
- Hand out flyers throughout your neighborhood, local stores, recreation facilities, churches, etc.
- Install open house signs with arrows at strategic points. Place colorful balloons on top of these signs. Put a colorful banner across your yard. The point is to draw as much attention to your home as possible.
- Have a register for people to sign in their name, phone number, and how they heard of your open house. Make this a requirement prior to a tour of your home.
- Follow up with calls asking their opinion of your home and if they have any suggestions to help you with selling it. People are generally anxious to give their opinion.

The Reality of Real Estate Investing

♦ To help you with your relationship with a Realtor and build up some trade off points. Give the list of potential buyers to your agent after you have determined they are not interested in your home, of course.

Neighborhood Canvassing

It is likely that someone in your neighborhood may know of a friend or relative they would like to live near them. Or, perhaps there is a renter who likes the area and now wants to become a home owner. Canvassing can be done in one of two ways:

1. Utilize the criss-cross directory as explained under open house tips. You can simply say, "I just wanted to let you know I have a nice home for sale in the neighborhood in case you may know of anyone who might be interested in buying. Do you happen to know of anyone?"
2. Print up nice flyers and distribute them through-out the neighborhood, door to door, at shopping centers, church and school gatherings, etc.

Bulletin Boards

In area grocery stores, libraries, recreation facilities, churches etc. you can put up your flyer and a photo, or use a 3 x 5 card to describe your home. There are also community bulletin boards on the internet.

Corporate Relocation Departments

Some corporate relocation departments put out monthly news letters to their employees throughout the country that include listings of homes for sale. Call the major corporate offices near your home and ask for the employee relocation department. Ask what advertising sources they have available for your home that is for sale.

Local Churches

Some religious communities also publish news letters that take advertisements. When possible I like to talk with the pastors to notify them of the home for sale. A new home owner in their area could also mean a new member of his church.

Qualifying Buyers

Show Your Home to Only Qualified Buyers

It is a real let down and a waste of time to show your home, enter into a contract, and then find out that the buyer does not even qualify to buy your home. Worse yet, you tie up your home for two months and then find out that the buyer cannot get the financing. Of course, nothing is 100% foolproof. However, you can certainly increase your chances for success by asking some questions and sometimes providing the buyer with some guidance to start with. This is especially important in working with a first time home buyer. Once you have answered the caller's questions and they have expressed an interest in seeing your home ask questions.

Questions to Ask

- Are you a first time home buyer? If the answer is no, ask, "Do you have a home to sell before you buy?" If they do, I will explain later how that can be OK.
- Are you a cash buyer, or do you need financing?
- Have you been pre-qualified by a loan officer?
- Two definitions are important for you to know at this point.

Pre-qualified - A loan officer asks a buyer what his income and expenses are, obtains his job history, and gets his social security number to run a credit report. This is not a full-blown, formal credit report. It is just a quick look to see if it appears that he is credit worthy. This information is obtained from only one bureau. There are no verifications. The loan officer takes him at his word at this point. This service is free. The loan officer usually spends between five to fifteen minutes talking to the potential buyer over the phone. Then he will generally get back to the buyer within twenty-four hours with his opinion of how much of a mortgage the buyer would qualify for. Depending on the amount of the down payment, they know what purchase price they should be looking at.

Pre-approved - A loan officer meets with the potential buyer face to face. A complete financial application is filled out at this time. This will require a fee, approximately $300, which covers the cost for an appraisal and a formal credit report. This is collected from the three major bureaus. Verifications are acquired, and the file is then gone over by an underwriter. It is the underwriter's job to determine who is approved or denied, or he may just ask for more documentation. Once approved, the buyer is given what is called a "Commitment Letter," but this states that the financing is still subject to an appraisal.

Now that you are clear on that be aware there are loan officers out there that will tell their buyers that they are pre-approved. They will give them a certificate stating they are pre-approved. However, in small print it will also state it is subject to verification of credit, income, etc. This is nothing more than a pre-qualification. The buyer generally does not know any better, but now you know that a true pre-approval is a commitment letter subject only to an appraisal.

♦ Do you know a loan officer, or may I refer one to you?

Many buyers will try to tell you that they will have no problem qualifying for financing. Maybe so; however, I learned the hard way when I first started to sell real estate. I had much of my time wasted. If they are not serious enough to take this step, then they are not really serious. Suggest to your prospective purchasers that to make the best use of their time and yours you would like them to be pre-qualified before showing them the home. This benefits them whether they buy your home or another home. There is no cost or obligation. The loan officer lets them know at what price level they qualify. The last thing you want to have happen is for them to fall in love with your home and then find out they cannot afford it. If the caller is unwilling to cooperate with this very reasonable request, say "Thank you for your inquiry; however, our attorney has advised us not to show our home to people we do not know who have not been at least pre-qualified." Do not let anyone talk you into side stepping this procedure. Those who try are the ones to avoid.

♦ What is the name and number of your loan officer?

You can call and verify the pre-qualification. Some loan officers provide the buyer a certificate; however, it usually does not state any thing specific. That is why I recommend that you talk directly to the loan officer to verify that he did look at the buyer's credit. Are there any possible problems? What is the amount of mortgage they can afford, etc.?

When a Buyer has a Home to Sell

What do you do when a buyer has to sell a home before closing on the purchase of yours? You certainly do not want to tie up your home waiting for them, hoping they can sell their home. However, you can still take advantage of this potential buyer. Your attorney or realtor will prepare a rider. Basically it will state that "This contract is subject to or contingent upon the sale of the buyer's home." I recommend that it should also state "The seller has the right to keep the home active on the market. If the seller gets another offer he wishes to accept, a 24-hour notice shall immediately be given to the buyer verbally and followed up with a fax or hard copy to drop the contingency and proceed to close on the purchase. If the buyer agrees to drop the contingency, he shall then provide proof of his ability to close within two weeks. This can be done by showing proof of funds with a bank statement or having the mortgage company provide a commitment letter. The buyer shall also deposit an additional thousand dollars earnest money." You need to pin the buyer down real tight because to move forward with him means to blow off your other offer. If the buyer does not or cannot drop his contingency, then he is out and the second buyer is in.

Here is another tip to be aware of when working with a realtor. The agent will commonly change the status of your home in the M.L.S. from active to contingency in situations like the above. Be sure to instruct your agent not to do this, to just keep it active. To satisfy the rules, tell the agent to add to the comments, "Weak contingency contract pending can be bumped with 24-hour notice." It is weak because the buyer cannot close without selling another home first. Some agents will not like doing this because it creates a little hassle for them. However, changing the status to contingency means you will get fewer showings. Some agents will not bother showing properties in contingent status. The whole idea, of course, is to maximize your selling efforts.

Your Financing Specialist

You will want to establish a relationship with a competent loan officer / broker, one that is not only knowledgeable and creative but also returns phone calls and follows up in a timely manner. Locating a loan officer is the same as for locating most professionals. Ask for referrals from your friends, relatives, church leader, realtor, attorney, etc.

When you first talk to loan officers, ask if they deal with B, C, and D paper? If they do not know what you are talking about, that is a tell-tale sign of their lack of experience in the business. B, C, and D paper simply refers to writing mortgages for people with credit problems, with D being the worst. Some loan officers specialize in this area. Their rates and points are higher because of the higher risk. They are still capable of doing A paper. Other loan officers focus on A and maybe a few B paper but do not want to bother with C and D paper. It is OK to work with either one. The main concern is, can they get the job done quickly and efficiently in taking care of all the buyers you refer to them. An A and B paper person should have a C and D paper person to whom you can refer your C and D paper buyers.

Let them know right up front where you are coming from and what you expect. You have a home to sell and when you have a buyer interested in seeing your home, you want them pre-qualified first. You want to know that when you give the loan officer a name and a number of a buyer that they will follow up immediately and report back to you. Ask how long it takes him to complete a pre-qualification. More than twenty four hours is not acceptable. When you have prospective buyers wanting to see your home they need to be pre-qualified and in your home as soon as possible.

To Hire an Attorney

We have all heard the jokes and wise cracks about attorneys. Let me include this one.

Once three professionals an accountant, a minister, and a lawyer - all provided services for an eccentric millionaire. One day he called all three to his beside and very weakly requested, "Since you are all trusted men in my service, I am entrusting you with envelopes containing one million dollars each. At the time of my death I want each of you to pass my coffin and drop the money in so that I will take it with me when I die and so my relatives will never discover where it went."

Within a week he was dead, and each professional passed by the coffin and, as instructed, dropped an envelope into the coffin. One year later the three met, and the accountant sheepishly confessed that he had taken his million dollars and placed an empty envelope into the coffin. He wanted to put the money to good use by helping out some relatives who were having financial problems and to build a homeless shelter.

The minister and lawyer told him he should not feel bad since he was helping out others in need. "As a matter of fact," said the minister, "I, too, placed an empty envelope into the coffin." He continued by saying, "As you know, I had a church that was falling apart; it had no heat and had a leaky roof. I spent the money for a new church."

Both the accountant and the lawyer relieved him of his guilty feelings since he was doing the work of God. Since it was the lawyer's turn to speak, the accountant and minister stared at him and finally asked, "Did you really put the money in the coffin as instructed?"

"But of course," said the lawyer. "And just to make sure it was safe, I took the cash out and put in my own personal check for one million dollars."

The same can probably be said about every profession out there. That is because dishonesty and incompetence exist in every profession. Also, some professionals who are competent just do not care about quality or fair and reasonable service. Fortunately there are very competent professionals out there who put high value on quality service.

Do you need to have an attorney represent you when buying or selling real estate? No. Do I recommend you hire an attorney? Yes, I do! Especially when you are still lacking in experience, a good attorney will save you more money than the fee he charges. Locating an attorney should not be difficult. Ask for recommendations from your friends, relatives, church leaders, realtor, loan officer, etc. Make sure the attorney has experience in handling real estate transactions. You do not want to pay for his training and acquiring experience.

Here is a referral already for you. They are competent in real estate and foreclosure laws. They are honest and dedicated to providing good quality service. If they were not, you can bet I would not be giving them a free plug here in my book! They have saved me much more money than the fees they have charged. They are located in downtown Chicago:

Kevin J. Hermanek 312-663-6665
Richard Shopiro 312-726-9060

CHAPTER 14

Negotiation

Literally from the time we start communicating we are negotiating. If you have children, you know exactly what I mean. You can never say no to a child just once because he will ask you for something over and over. Sometimes they find different ways to ask for the same thing. They do not take "no" for an answer. I know with my own children, even though I am on to it, once in a while it works for them.

School age children negotiate with their teachers over their assignments, homework, etc. As adults we negotiate with our friends, co-workers, bosses, and spouses constantly everyday. Who is going to do this or that? Can I do this or that? We are constantly negotiating.

Negotiation is the art of focusing on gaining the favor of people from whom we want things. It is the power of influencing someone to make a specific decision. It is as simple as that. You know you have negotiated well when you get a good deal for yourself and the other party is smiling because they feel they also got a good deal. It is a win / win scenario. Negotiation is not taking advantage of someone or taking them for all they have. That is just being a bully. I have seen situations where people have pushed an owner in foreclosure so far, making the deal sweeter for themselves and negotiating themselves right out of a deal. I can not tell you specifically how to gauge when you are asking too much. That is something you learn through experience and feel out in each individual deal. Just know that you need to strive to leave the other party with the ability to make a fresh start. You have to leave them with some dignity. Remember - win / win!

Negotiating Tips / Building Rapport

Be friendly! From the very beginning you are building rapport. Gather facts about the seller's circumstances that you will use in structuring a deal with him. In the beginning one of the first questions you will be asking is, "What have you already been doing to solve your problem? What is it that you would like to have happen?" They will talk about keeping the home or about getting rid of it. This will give you a direction to work towards. Once you have sufficient facts you will know if you can help them accomplish their desires. If not, then you will play the role of counselor in helping them to face the reality of their situation and guide them towards a decision.

The First Offer

Your first offer should always be lower than what you really would consider paying for the property. You could get lucky and get a better price than you were expecting or you are allowing yourself room to negotiate up. The ideal situation is if you can get the seller to first tell you what he is willing to take. This happens with rapport building. You really do not have any idea what number the seller is thinking. Sometimes it is a number lower than your number. When possible let the seller tell you what he is thinking. It might be just $1,000 to help him with moving expenses while you are thinking possibly of giving him $5,000 for his equity. Let the seller give the number first!

Never appear anxious. Let sellers know you have two other deals you are also considering, but you are interested in their property however, if it does not work out, you will buy one of the other properties you are currently looking at. When talking in general and building rapport, you can try some feeler questions like, *"If someone were able to, or if someone offered you, would you consider it?"* Using the "if" word is the key word here. It does not create any obligation and the answer gives you a good indication what the seller is thinking. Always maintain your walk-away power. You cannot allow yourself to get emotionally involved with the property. Do not fall in love with it. If you do, you are likely to pay more than you need to, and you may buy yourself right into no profit. I have seen it happen too often. When it does not seem that you are going to be able to make it happen at a reasonable profit for your time and investment, say, "Well, it looks like we will not be able to do business after all, Mr. Seller; good luck to you." Then get up and walk out. Start working on your next deal. When the seller sees how serious you are, he may not let you get out the door.

When to Stop Talking

When you make an offer to someone, do not continue talking, trying to explain, or justifying your position. Just keep quiet! Wait for the seller's response. In most cases you already know there is good reason for motivation, especially if you found out about the property through the foreclosure sources. The only question in your mind is whether you can get the seller to agree to your price or terms. Remain quiet until you hear the seller's response. It may seem like a long time; it may be uncomfortable. However, he who speaks first usually loses; so be quite!

Higher Authority / Good Guy - Bad Guy

I have always found the best strategy is pretend that I have a financial partner who makes the final decisions, or that I am the manager for the investor who bought the property. You see, this way you can never be pressured into making a decision or be put on the spot because you simply put it off onto your higher authority. When tenants try to get away with paying the rent late, then you can tell them the owner simply has no flexibility when it comes to paying the rent late. Since you are required to file eviction right away, "What can we do to get the rent in on time?" Or you can say your financing partner is really firm on how much he is willing to allow you to offer and he just will not budge. He is the bad guy, and you are the sympathetic go between. In that role a seller or tenant will tend to say more to you than he otherwise would.

How do you avoid having the higher authority tactic used on yourself? When you are making an appointment, confirm with the party you are dealing with that he has the authority to make the deal. You can say, "If I am able to make an offer that is reasonable, do you have the authority to make a decision to accept or reject it?" If not, then tell the seller you will need to meet with him and his wife, or father-in-law, or whoever it might be who does have the authority. You should also ask if any other names are on the title and that you want to meet with them as well. When you are in the midst of a negotiation and you feel the good guy / bad guy tactic is being used on you, simply say, with a slight chuckle in your voice, "You are not going to use the good guy / bad guy tactic on me, are you? Tell you what, from now on anything you tell me he says, I will interpret as you saying it."

The Initial Walk Through

In a non-offensive way be sure to point out all the negative features and repairs. Surely the owner is aware of them. However having lived with them for some time, they have gotten used to them and hardly notice them anymore. Help him to see these as a first time home buyer would. This helps to dissolve the pie-in-the-sky figure they may be thinking of and bring them down to reality.

Emotional Outbursts

Do not shy away from emotional outburst like crying, just be there. Listen to their problems, sometimes you will get an ear full. Be sympathetic. All this is quite important in building rapport with the owner. The better you can do this, the more deals you will make. When the emotional outburst is anger being displayed, do not push your luck, use good judgement. a soothing comment may be helpful at this point like; "Things can only get better, and I am here to see if I can help make them better!" If the anger displayed makes you uncomfortable excuse yourself by saying something like; "Perhaps this is not a good time, may I call upon you again tomorrow?" Otherwise, just turn around and leave. I have never had a bad experience. The worst is probably when I knocked on a door and the man made some rude remark and demanded me off his property. Then he followed behind me to my car and watched me drive away.

The Stall

When the owner just will not make a decision or he asks for time to think it over, this is stalling. Sometimes you have to guide him to a decision. See Case in Point # 12, Evergreen Park. You need to reassure him, repeat the benefits for him, that time is of the essence, and explain that this is a win / win solution for him and you. Ask if he believes you. If he say yes, repeat that time is short; *"Why not start resolving this right now so you can start looking toward the future"*. If he says no or hesitates, making it obvious he has concerns, then push gently further to get to the specific reasons. Then answer those reservations.

The Better Offer

Sometimes the owner will tell you another investor has made him a better offer. Ask what it is; then congratulate him and wish him good luck! You hope it all works out well. Ask if the other person who has made this better offer has asked for any money up front from the seller. As I mentioned earlier in a previous chapter, there are unscrupulous characters out there who will scam people in foreclosure. Certainly you should warn them of this. Tell them to have their attorney check it out first for legitimacy. Some investors will give them a highball offer, leading them on, burning up their time until it is too late, and the property goes to auction. Advise him to be careful, check it out, and to call you if it does not work out.

Split the Difference

Some negotiating has been taking place, and now the buyer and seller are close to an agreement but neither wants to budge any further. For example, lets us say the buyer is at $52,000 and the seller is at $56,000. It could be either party; let's make you the buyer, and you say something like, *"Gee we are only $4,000 apart. Surely we are not going to kill the deal over $4,000 dollars! Tell you what,* *how about we split the difference? You come down $2,000 and we will come up $2,000. What do you say?"* The seller gives in, *"Great! So you are willing to take $54,000. I will go and see if I can convince my financial partner to agree to $54,000. I will talk to you tomorrow."* Tomorrow comes, and you are ready to talk to the seller again. You say, *"I am so embarrassed. I thought for sure I would be able to get my partner to go along with the $54,000. We went over and over the numbers last night and my financial partner just could not see us paying any more than $51,000."* After the seller's negative response, you say, *"I understand how you feel, but gee now we are only $1,000 apart. Surely we are not going to kill the deal over $1,000. What can we do? We are only $1,000 apart."* You keep this up and the seller may offer to split the difference again. If not, you can say, *"if you will agree to split the difference and come down $500 to $51,500, I guarantee we'll have a deal, because I'll put up the $500 out of my pocket if I have to. What do you say, can we wrap up this deal right now?"* More often than not the seller will agree.

The Art of Flinching

Flinching is your response and your willingness to question the price when it is given. It is not done directly, but in such a way that the person giving it knows that the amount is not acceptable. For example, the car salesman is trained to look to see if a customer flinches. When someone asks, "What is the price?" The salesman gives it and observes the response - both verbally and in body language. If it appears the price seemed good or had no negative response from the prospective buyer, then the salesman moves on in a different direction to close the sale. However, if the buyer's eyebrows raised up, eyes got real big, and or the buyer said something like, "Wow! I would never pay that much!" The salesman then might say in a whispered tone while taking a step closer something like, *"I am sure if you make an offer, we can negotiate the sales manager down on the price."* When the sales manager gives the number that he says is the best deal he can give the buyer, and the buyer again flinches and decides to exercise walk-away power by heading for the door, the sales manager says, *"All right, all right, if you buy tonight, I can give it to you for $100 over invoice.* (For your information I have personally bought several new cars for $100 over invoice and once for $25 over invoice. The dealer gets something like 5% back from the manufacturer; so it is not as though they are only making $100 although they let you think that if you do not know any better.) By the way, have the dealer show you the actual invoice.

The flinching technique works in all kinds of situations.

The next time your child or spouse asks for some extra spending money for something, even if you are willing to give the amount asked for, try flinching.

Allen Watkins

See if he / she does not come back at you with, "OK, then how about $__ instead."

When a potential seller first gives you his asking price, flinch by saying something like, "$79,000! Oh, I could never, or I know my partner would never pay that price!" Then wait and hear his response. Right away he is likely to tell you *"Well, that price is negotiatable."*

Divorcing Owners

It can be a little tricky dealing with two owners who are sometimes literally at war with each other. However, it can be done. Remember you must remain neutral at all times. You can never side with or agree with one spouse against another. If you do, you will lose all hope of making a deal.

- ♦ Always get both signatures and get them notarized.

- ♦ Provide each with his own copy of the paperwork.

- ♦ Never give money to one for the other. Write checks to each for their agreed upon amount.

The Loan Extension

Sometimes the buyer's closing date arrives before the approval for their loan. It could be because they dragged their feet in getting some of the documents requested by the loan officer. It could be because the loan officer or the processor did not order the appraisal soon enough, or the appraiser is taking extra long in getting the report done. It could be for numerous other reasons. The main fact of the matter is, that you are the one at risk. If the deal falls through, you have lost valuable time. Now you are being asked to extend the agreed upon time. It is not your fault; however, it is all your risk. Granting the extension the way the buyer, agent, and perhaps your attorney have presented it to you is not fair, in my opinion. Should the buyer's financing end up still falling through, does this extension agreement compensate you for all your lost time? Probably not!

I suggest you request that the buyer sign for and release the earnest money, or at least an amount equal to your cost for the property during the entire financing period. That means you can take the money and do with it whatever you want because it is yours. If the buyer still closes, of course it is credited towards the purchase. If not, the buyer has lost it as liquidated damages to you for not completing the purchase. This technique will show the seriousness of the buyer, and, after all, the risk should be his instead of yours. If the buyer refuses to sign over the earnest money to you, then do not agree to an extension. Instead, explain that the property will go back on the market. When the buyer has an approval and is ready to close, then you will allow the buyer to still close at the original agreed upon amount. However, if you get an offer in the interim, you are free to accept it without notice, and the first buyer is out. Of course, realtors will not like this technique. Expect resistance, and gently insist on doing what is in your best interest.

The Right to Resell the Deal

There are plenty of individuals who lack money who are out there writing offers on properties, closing and making money anyway. They accomplish this by selling their contract to someone else. You maintain this option for yourself by always signing your name and then including the words "and or nominee." This is perfectly legitimate. The seller still gets what was agreed to. However, when objections come up, you might say:

- "I am not sure if the title will be in my name, or my spouse's, (or my partner's) name."
- "I might decide to place title in a Land Trust."

The First Right of Refusal

The "First Right of Refusal" is the technique of saying to the seller when it becomes apparent that he is just not going to come down to your price, "Mr seller it looks like we are just not going to be able to agree upon a price today. Could you do this for me, give me the First Right of Refusal?" Then go on to explain to the seller what it means. "It just basically means that should you get another offer from someone else, that you will give me the chance to match or beat the offer before you accept it." If you can get it in writing. Not that you would actually enforce it however, by it being in writing will help the seller remember to call you first before accepting another offer. Over time after you have moved on chasing other deals and forgotten about this one, the seller may become more flexible and call you with an acceptable deal.

These negotiating techniques really work. They can save you money. They can help you make money. Study them, and, most important, use them!

Business not Emotional Decisions

Do not allow yourself to fall in love with a property that you have to have at any cost. If you do it will usually be a great cost, in time and money! I have seen people get all caught up in their emotions thinking "I just need to have this property!" That they over extend themselves financially, before they know it they have created an alligator. Love soon turns into hate and their investment career is terminated or at a minimum postponed. I have seen it happen at auctions, through my brokerage business in contract negotiations when there is more than one offer on a property and the seller is playing the buyers against each other. At one auction I witnessed a man who was known as an experienced respected investor, get flustered bidding against a woman who appeared to be a home buyer. His emotions of disgust with his competition were displayed. It was like he felt "How dare this home buyer bid against me!" Well he jumped the bidding quite high and probably broke even or took a loss on the deal.

You need to be business minded, it is about numbers not because you really like the appearance of the property and can not wait to show it to your wife and friends and declare; "Look at what I own!"

Be patient, do not let yourself get overly anxious feeling; "I just need to get this next deal," and do not allow yourself to become discouraged because other people keep out bidding you. Accept the fact that you will be out bid a lot more than being the successful bidder. The competition can not always be there, as long as you remain consistent and persistent your deals will happen. Recently, I went to an auction to bid on three different homes. I was hopeful that I would win the bidding on all three of them, or at least one. As it turned out, I was out bid on all three. Disappointing, sure it was however, I had predetermined what my limit would be and that is where I stopped. My money was still safe in my bank account waiting for the next deal.

The next auction I was prepared to bid on five properties. I got out bid on two, bid up and won on two, and the third I got for $10,500, there were no other bidders. This was the best property out of all of them. A nice brick two unit, occupied with tenants who had let me in prior to the sale. It had nice oak cabinets in the kitchens and baths. Needed only minor repairs and a new roof. The value $47,000 and the monthly income $775 which I collected the first time three weeks later. Why did no one else bid on it? Because no one else took the time to follow up on that address, except me. The important point here is, had I won the bids at the previous auction I would of probably been tied up and not followed up on this auction. Patience paid off. That is what I want you to remember. Wait for the right deal, do not get over anxious and pay more than you should for a property. Let the other guys do that.

CHAPTER 15

Get Motivated

We are born into this life naked; we also leave naked. What we do in between is tremendously important. Although we cannot take our material assets with us, we do take what cannot be bought with all the money in the world. We take our Peace of Mind! Or, we take our War of Mind! I believe this is literally hell for some who have already passed on. Have you ever had an opportunity to do something and chosen not to and then later regretted it? Now, magnify that regret a million times.

You see, this life that we have is a precious gift that we have been given. I believe we are expected to make the most of it. The knowledge obtained in this book is about taking a negative situation involving real estate and turning it into a positive one, and earning money while doing so. In some cases a great amount of money may be earned. We have all heard that money is the root of all evil; however, money can be the root for much good, also. It really depends on the people who possess it and how they use it. Certainly the opportunities for doing good are multiplied for the man or woman who has it, versus the man or woman who does not. Even so, just earning money is not what it is all about. Consider building a strong moral character (Now, that we take with us!) which encompasses spirituality, friendships, family, doing good for all mankind, etc.

To achieve a truly successful life means striving for a balance of all that is good and praiseworthy in the development of our character. Even though we take it with us when we leave this life, we also leave it behind in our reputation and the influence we have had on other lives. For good or for bad, once our life opportunity has passed, it cannot be changed. It cannot be taken from us!

To make the most of our lives, we need a game plan, a road map. We need goals! Some people spend more time planning a vacation than they do their lives.

You must systematically decide what it is that you want to accomplish. You must have a specific end in mind.

Goals

Spencer W. Kimball: *"We do believe in setting goals. We live by goals. In athletics we always have a goal. When we go to school, we have the goal of graduation and degrees. Our total existence is goal-oriented."*

Allen Watkins

"We must have goals to make progress, encouraged by keeping records — as the swimmer or the jumper or the runner does. Progress is easier when it is timed, checked, and measured. Goals are good. Laboring with a distant aim sets the mind in a higher key and puts us at our best. Goals should always be made to a point that will make us reach and strain."

"It is most appropriate for [you] ... to quietly, and with determination, set some serious personal goals in which [you] ... will seek to improve by selecting certain things that [you] ... will accomplish within a specified period of time. Even if [you] ... are headed in the right direction, if [you] ... are ... without momentum [you] ... will have too little influence."

As a general rule, it is much better to focus on a few pertinent goals at one time rather than attempting to focus on many goals simultaneously. Use wisdom in determining how many goals you attempt to focus on at the same time, according to your particular temperament, ability, etc.

Goals, of course, need to be realistic, something you are not currently achieving, and something that will require a certain amount of mental and perhaps physical exertion. Your goals must not be too easy to achieve, or you will be falling short of your potential.

Select goals in every facet of your life, not just goals related to earning money. You are entitled to achieve your ultimate potential, be it emotionally, socially, spiritually, professionally, or academically oriented. Approach everything you desire to achieve with a steadfastness of purpose.

Goals are good for us. They make us reach and strain. Consistently setting and accomplishing new goals is necessary to living a full life. We have all heard the stories of people accomplishing their goal of retiring. Some wither and die within a few short years. Others go on to live active and productive lives well into their nineties and beyond. Why? It is because of their attitude and mind-set. They have new horizons to see, new mountains to climb, and just simply, new goals to accomplish. A person does not have to plan to fail or wither away. However, one must plan to succeed to have a full, productive life.

You must maintain a committed, determined effort in order for your goal to be achieved. Remember, desires are merely wishes unless you back your desires with effort. Your success in achieving your goal will be in direct proportion to your efforts, not your circumstances. When you come upon a road block, face it with the determination to go over it, around it, under it, or right through it! Where there is a will, there is a way!

First, prepare to write down your plan. Start with your dream list. What are the things that motivate you? Are they a new home, a car, a nice vacation for your family, the financial ability to help others, the financial freedom to be able to devote more time to being a good husband and father, etc., etc., etc. Anything

The Reality of Real Estate Investing

ever accomplished or created by anyone in existence was first a thought, and then it was written down.

Write out your business plan / goals. It is important to be specific! What will you do? What will it take to accomplish the things on your dream list? Accept the fact that you will constantly be re-evaluating your progress and making revisions to your plan. By doing so, you will continue to move forward.

Some categories to consider in planning for improvement and goal setting are: personal, family, spiritual, and business. Again, it is important to be specific!

Write out how much money you want to be earning per month by the end of the first year, second year, and third year. Write out a specific plan for the time commitment and activities that will be necessary to accomplish this. Plan it on a daily, weekly, and monthly basis. It begins with the first day and goes one day at a time from that point on.

Napoleon Hill: *"There is a difference between wishing for a thing and being ready to receive it. No one is ready for a thing until he believes he can acquire it. The state of mind must be belief, not mere hope or wish. Open-mindedness is essential for belief. Closed minds do not inspire faith, courage, and belief."*

"Remember, no more effort is required to aim high in life, to demand abundance and prosperity, than is required to accept misery and poverty."

The power of faith has power, dominion, and authority over all things. Learn to approach everything you desire to achieve with the power of faith in mind.

Exert Yourself Mentally

The thought process itself is the key to exercising faith. To a great extent we accomplish what we think about. What we think about today, tomorrow, or next month will mold our attitudes and determine what we will accomplish during our lives. Our life is influenced more by our thoughts than anything else.

Spencer W. Kimball: *"How could a person possibly become what he is not thinking? Nor is any thought, when persistently entertained, too small to have its effect. The divinity that shapes our ends is indeed in ourselves."*

In order to exercise faith, once we have selected a righteous desire (e.g. increasing our earning power, helping a friend with a problem, etc.), we must become pre-occupied with our desire. Faith can be gauged to a great extent by the amount of time spent thinking about our righteous desire. If our mind is not pre-occupied with the thing we are trying to achieve, it is not a desire.

Do not confuse the pre-occupation of worry and anxiety with the pre-occupation involved in exercising faith. When our minds are prone to dwell on the adverse consequences of events, which we assume we have very little control over, that is worry. In contrast, if our minds dwell on the possible consequences of various courses of action which we will control to a great extent, we are exercising faith.

Grant Von Harrison: *"The mind is like a field. We will harvest whatever we plant in it, if it is nourished."*

Research has demonstrated that most people use their minds in constructive thinking only about ten per cent of the time. Similarly, the amount of faith they exercise is extremely limited.

Joseph Smith: *"Where doubt and uncertainty are there faith is not, nor can it be. For doubt and faith do not exist in the same person at the same time; so that persons whose minds are under doubt and fears cannot have unshaken confidence; and where unshaken confidence is not, there faith is weak."*

Thinking negatively does not require any effort; maintaining a believing frame of mind, however, requires an exerted effort over a sustained period of time. By the process of faith, thoughts produce an effect as literal as physical exertion. Your thoughts, more than anything else, will be the determining factor in what you accomplish during your life.

Your Mind's Eye

One of the best ways to exert yourself mentally is to create a mental picture of the thing for which you are striving, and to repeatedly bring this picture to mind. In a very literal sense, desired ends must be created spiritually in the mind before they can be realized. If you have ever planted seeds for a garden or a flower bed, didn't you visualize in your mind's eye what the plant would look like when it was grown, such as a tomato plant or a beautiful flower?

Seeing things in your mind's eye is seeing with the "eye of faith." See or visualize in your mind's eye yourself looking at homes and evaluating their investment potential. See yourself making an offer and having it accepted. Now see yourself holding the deed of ownership to the property.

We must first think it and visualize it before we can achieve it.

Napoleon Hill: *"Whatever the mind of man can conceive and believe, it can achieve!"*

Auto Suggestion

Here is a most significant fact: the subconscious mind takes any orders given it in a spirit of absolute faith and acts upon those orders, although the orders often have to be presented over and over again through repetition before they are interpreted by the subconscious mind.

Prepare a written statement of your desire through which you are endeavoring to develop a money consciousness. Remember that the mere reading of the words is of no consequence unless you mix emotion or feeling with your words. Your subconscious mind recognizes and acts only upon thoughts which have been well mixed with emotion or feeling.

Through repetition of the following exercise you voluntarily create thought habits which are favorable to your efforts to transmute desire into its monetary equivalent.

First: Go into some quiet spot (preferably in bed at night) where you will not be disturbed or interrupted, close your eyes, and repeat aloud (you need to hear your own words) the written statement of the amount of money you intend to accumulate, the time limit for its accumulation, and a description of the effort you intend to give in return for the money. As you carry out these instructions, see yourself already in possession of the money.

For example: Suppose you intend to accumulate $50,000 by the end of six months from today. You intend to read and re-read this book and other books of a positive, motivational nature. You see yourself devoting specific time periods of your day for reading. You intend to apply the knowledge and techniques and see yourself researching, driving by properties, evaluating them, contacting owners, contacting prospective investors, preparing other creative financial avenues, attending auctions, bidding, winning the bid, etc. The written statement of your purpose should be similar to the following: *"By the 10th of October I will have in my possession $50,000, which will come to me in various amounts from time to time during the interim. In return for this money I will give the most efficient and dedicated effort of which I am capable, in developing a systematic approach to researching out information on properties by re-reading this book while I am actually performing the procedures of going through the newspapers for legal notices, researching the court files, driving by properties, knocking on doors, talking with owners, touring their homes, preparing and presenting offers, and bidding at auctions. I will continue doing this until I get an offer accepted or win a bid at the auction. I will then pay for the property with cash that I have obtained through an investor or from cash advances from credit cards, lines of credit, or any of the many other creative financing sources available to me. I will frame on the wall a copy of the deed of ownership of my first property."*

Then describe your plans to rent and refinance or resell and the actions to accomplish the same. Keep going until you receive the money in your hands. State: *"I believe that I will have this money in my possession. My faith is so strong that I can now see this money before my eyes. I can touch it with my hands. It is now waiting transfer to me once I follow through with my plan."*

Second: Repeat this program morning and night until you can see with your mind's eye the money you intend to accumulate.

Third: Carry a written copy of your statement with you and refer to it regularly until it has been memorized.

As you carry out these instructions, remember you are carrying out the principles of auto-suggestion for the purpose of giving orders to your subconscious mind.

Top professional athletes use auto-suggestion to improve their performance.

Remember also, that your subconscious mind will act only upon instructions that are emotionalized and handed over to it with "feeling." Faith is the strongest and most productive of the emotions. The time will soon come, if you do as you have been instructed in spirit as well as in action, when a whole new universe of power will unfold to you.

The Challenge

The biggest challenge you are going to have in your pursuit of success at real estate investing is defeating the enemies of success.

Discouragement

Your biggest adversary is **Discouragement**. It will come at you from many different directions. Some sources of discouragement you can usually depend on are:

- family members
- close friends
- acquaintances
- even people you do not know, as the leads you contact

Discouragement also comes in many forms. Some well-meaning family members and friends will bring it to you in what they feel is advice or encouragement not to pursue your dreams. Of course, when you look at what they have accomplished in their lives, you think, *"Who are they to give me advice?"*

Rejection is another form that discouragement uses. Prepare yourself for and accept the fact that you are going to hear "No" much more than "Yes." That is a fact! I have been there; done it! It is a numbers game! Develop the mentality, "For every no I get, I am getting closer to a yes!"

Consistent, persistent effort is the key ingredient to achieving success in over-coming the enemies and winning the war! It only happens if you make it happen! It is important for that concept to stick. **"It only happens if you make it happen!"** Do not think, "Can hardly wait till I get a lucky break." **You make your own luck!**

You will have moments of despair and discouragement. It is during these moments that you need to fight the hardest. I have seen many succumb to its enticing. It will tell you, "Why are you working so hard? You are just wasting your time. You were not meant to have success. Just settle for less. Give it up. You will be happier!"

It is during these times that you need to reach deep down inside yourself and focus on your desires and dreams!

A famous national speaker **Les Brown** shares a personal experience: *When I was a boy, I sold used television sets door to door in my neighborhood with my buddy Bou. Bou and I discovered that selling door to door can be cruel and unusual punishment. I'd go up to a door, knock on it, and politely say, "Hello, would you like to buy a nice working television set?"*

"No!" And the door would slam in my face. BAM! The first time Bou had that happen, he headed back to his car. "I can't do this," he said. But I couldn't go back to the car. My Mama was ill at that time. She couldn't work; I was hungry, literally hungry. I couldn't afford to quit, so I kept going. That's a powerful motivation. I've known people who have deliberately put themselves in a **"can't afford to quit"** *position just to make sure they stayed on track to their goals.*

I discovered back then on the door to door route that when you step into your fears and continue to push yourself, something happens to you. You develop courage. I kept on — from one door to the next. "No!" BAM! "No!" BAM! "No!" BAM! You know what? After awhile, I no longer took it personally. I began to play a game. I thought there must be a "yes" out there somewhere, and I decided that I wasn't going home until I found one.

And eventually somebody did say "yes!" and I said, "I knew I would find you!"

Never, never, never, take rejection personally. They do not even know you. If they did know you, they would say, "Yes!" You know you have a legitimate, viable answer to their problem. Actually, if you cannot solve their problem, you will simply be able to help them by lending a listening ear and at least explaining the foreclosure process to them. Believe me, they do not know because no one before has taken the time to explain it to them. Sometimes they are sitting there worrying that the eviction might be happening any day, when actually they may have several months. Be confident. You have something worthwhile to offer to them, even if they slam the door in your face. It is their loss. Sometimes it requires a little creativity to get through. Once, after not getting any response to three notes I had left at a property, I left a note stating, "Sorry to keep bothering you. However, I can not stop trying until I hear from you. My wife's orders. Please help me out by calling me. "I got a call the next day. He told me that after that statement, he just had to call. And I did make a deal with him. See Case in Point # 19, Mohawk.

Procrastination

Another formidable foe is procrastination. Some people think procrastination is funny; however, it is no laughing matter. It has been the cause of many lost battles. It frustrates even the most highly motivated people. It keeps them from achieving their ambitions, no matter how hard they strive. It causes untold guilt, anxiety, and anguish.

Your best battle stratagem is to refer to your goals again.

They can not be vague goals. That would be trying to win a war using guns with blanks. You must make your goals tangible. You do this by being specific and making the goal something you can draw or visualize. It includes reading legal notices, knocking on the door of the property, talking to the home owner, etc. Have several small goals that lead up to your desired results.

Procrastination may be nothing more than a defense mechanism to not do something you do not want to deal with. It may be fear of failure. It may be fear of success, or it may be anxiety that others may think you are doing too well.

The best tactical maneuver is to remain focused on small specific goals. This will counter the "all or nothing" approach that can be an obstacle. One step, one goal at a time. You can not win the war until you have won several battles first!

Motivation

You must be motivated! To what level of motivation are you committed?

Dictionary definition

Wish: to have a longing for; want
Desire: to long for; crave

My definition of a wish: It is like a half hearted dream. A person may say "I wish I could play a piano like Liberace, or Elton John, or hit a baseball like Sammy Sosa or Mark McQuire, or play basketball like Michael Jordan or Larry Bird. However, unless he is willing to put in the time and effort, years of hard work and practice, his wish is only a half hearted dream.

My definition of desire: It is like a dream you visualize in your minds eye, and require to become a reality so much, that you put forth effort no matter how hard, to make it so.

Did you know that when Larry Bird was a boy, he was just a skinny little kid with very little athletic ability. However, he had a desire to be one of the best basketball players that had ever lived. Larry Bird had so much desire that he would get up at 5:00 AM every morning, go to the gym and practice his basketball skills. He practiced relentlessly! What did not come to him in natural ability he developed by pure persistent hard work and practice. He had true desire!

Now you may be thinking "come on Allen I am not trying to accomplish anything great, I just want to make more money." Well, I understand that, however, the same principle applies, you can wish for more money, or you can desire it!

You are reading my book because you at least have a wish for something more. My desire is that if your wish is merely a wish, that I can help spark you into making your wish a burning desire!

There was once a Roman general who realized the importance of motivation as he was about to send his reluctant troops into a battle in which they were greatly out numbered. The general knew his men would have to be highly motivated to win, but they were not. So, after his army had sailed to the enemy's land and disembarked on the hostile shore, he gave the order for his OWN ships to be burned. The general then commanded his troops, "We win, or we die!" With that strong motivation they won.

Failure is the result of one's LACK of consistent,
persistent effort.

**Success is the result of
CONSISTENT,
PERSISTENT EFFORT.**

Attitude
By Charles Swindell

*"The longer I live, the more I realize the impact of attitude on life. Attitude, to me, is more important than facts. It is more important that the past, than education, than money, than circumstances, than failure, than successes, than whatever people think or say or do. It is more important than appearances, giftedness, or skill. It will make or break a company ... a church ... a home. The remarkable thing is we have a choice every day regarding the attitude we will embrace for that day. We cannot change our past ... we cannot change the fact that people will act in a certain way. We cannot change the inevitable. The only thing we can do is play on the one string we have, and that is our attitude ... I am convinced that life is 10 percent what happens to me and **90 percent how I react to it**. And so it is with you ... we are in charge of our 'attitudes.' Attitude is everything!!!"*

Don't Quit

When things go wrong, as they sometimes will,
When the road you're trudging seems all uphill,
When the funds are low and the debts are high,
And you want to smile, but you have to sigh,
   When care is pressing you down a bit,
   Rest if you must, but don't you quit.
   Life is queer with its twists and turns,
   As every one of us sometimes learns,
   And many a fellow turns about
When he might have won had he stuck it out.
Don't give up though the pace seems slow,
   You may succeed with another blow.
   Often the goal is nearer than it seems
   to a faint and faltering man.
   Often the struggler has given up
when he might have captured the victor's cup,
And he learned too late when the night came down,
   How close he was to the victor's crown.
   Success is failure turned inside out,
   The silver tint of the clouds of doubt.
   And you never can tell how close you are;
   It may be near when it seems afar.
So stick to the fight when you're hardest hit,
It's when things seem worst that you mustn't quit!
               (Author unknown)

It is far better to attempt something great and fail,
   than to do nothing and succeed!

Allen Watkins

You

You are the one who has to decide,
Whether you'll do it or toss it aside.
You are the one who makes up your mind,
Whether you'll lead or linger behind —
Whether you'll try for the goal that's afar,
Or just be content to stay where you are.
Take it or leave it. Here's something to do!
Just think it over. It's all up to you!
Nobody will compel you to rise.
No one will force you to open your eyes.
No one will answer for you, yes or no,
Whether to stay there or whether to go.
Life is a game, but it's you who must say,
Whether as cheat or as sportsman you'll play.
Fate may betray you, but you settle first,
Whether to live to your best or your worst.
So whatever it is you're wanting to be,
Remember to fashion the choice you are free.
Kindly or selfish or gentle or strong,
Keeping the right way or taking the wrong,
Careless of honor or guarding your pride.
All these are questions which you must decide.
Yours the selection, whichever you do,

Success or Failure, it's all up to you.
(Author unknown)

The Reality of Real Estate Investing

"If you think you can't or if you think you can, you are right!"

Willie Mae Jones is a 37-year old devoted homemaker and mother. She lives in a rural country town in Alabama. She found herself traveling in her old pick-up truck one evening down a country road to visit a friend. Her 8-year old son Rocky was with her. Tired from his day of activities, he had stretched out on the front seat and rested his feet on his mom's lap.

As she continued down the road, she came to a one-lane bridge. Downshifting, she started to proceed across the bridge. Just then the left front wheel hit a large pothole. The truck swerved. Willie Mae attempted to compensate to prevent the truck from going off the bridge, but Rocky's feet got caught in the steering wheel, and off the bridge the truck tumbled. Smashing nose down on the side of the embankment, it then rolled over and over until it stopped upside down at the bottom of the 75-foot gully. The driver's side of the cab was crushed down to the dashboard. Willie Mae had suffered a laceration that ran from her mouth to her right eyebrow; two teeth had been knocked out; her left collar bone and arm were broken; and a bone was sticking out of her arm pit.

Miraculously Rocky was uninjured. It was dark, but he could see the truck's tires spinning in the moonlight. *"Mom,"* he said, *"Why are the tires spinning up in the air?"* There was no reply. *"Mom! Mom! Wake up!"*

She muttered, *"...sleep."* It was quite agonizing for her to speak.

Rocky again said, *"No, Mom, wake up! Wake up!"* Realizing now that they had been in a bad accident, Rocky felt the need to get his mom out of the truck and go for help. He coaxed his mother over and over to wake up and begin to move. He pulled and tugged until he got her out of the truck. Once out of the truck she tried to lie down. Rocky said, *"No, Mom, we must go up the hill for help."*

"Let me sleep," she replied.

Rocky said, *"No, Mom, let's go!"* With her good arm around his shoulder they began their climb. Willie Mae was in unbearable pain, and she felt the uncontrollable urge to want to go to sleep. Every couple of steps she would stumble and say, *"...sleep,"* but Rocky insisted they keep going. Soon he remembered the story his mom had read to him about the little engine that could. The engine had struggled just as he was now struggling to climb the hill. Rocky began to chant, *"I think I can; I think I can; I know I can; I know I can!"* He kept this up until they finally reached the top. Willie Mae fell to her knees. From a distance a car's headlights were coming their way. Rocky could now see his mom more clearly. He began to cry, *"Oh, Mom, you are hurt so bad."* He flagged down the car.

Willie Mae received 256 sutures in her face along with some reconstructive surgery to her mouth. Her fractured shoulder is healed now, and she is one proud mother. She knows if it had not been for her son's encouraging words, she would not have survived. Rocky was heralded as a hero. He says, *"I only did what anyone would have done."*

"If you think you can't or if you think you can, you are right!" Henry Ford

> The difference between a winner and a loser is simple;
> a quitter never wins and
> **a winner never quits!**

The Key To Success

Once there was a college student pondering his meaning in life. More than anything else he wanted to be a success. *"But how do I become a success?"* he thought. *"What do I need to do? What is the key to success?"*

Shortly thereafter he attended a seminar taught by the great philosopher Socrates. Being very impressed by Socrates words he thought, *"Now there is someone who can give me some insight into the key to success."*

When the seminar was over, he found Socrates outside on the steps talking with a group of students. He walked up to him, tapped Socrates on the shoulder, and said, *"Socrates, what is the key to success?"* Socrates quickly glanced in the direction of the young man, then turned back and continued his conversation with the group. The young man thought, *"Maybe he didn't hear me."* He tapped Socrates on the shoulder a little harder and said a little louder, *"Socrates, what is the key to success?"* Socrates turned, looked him right in the eye, and then turned back around and continued talking with the group of students. Now the young man was getting a little offended, and he shouted, *"Socrates, what is the key to success?"* Socrates turned around quickly, stared right into the young man's eyes, and said, *"Follow me!"* He started walking across the school grounds. When he got to the parking lot, he looked over his shoulder and the young man was following close behind. He continued past the parking lot and off the school grounds. He walked up to the bottom of a large hill, looked over his shoulder and the young man was still following close behind. He walked to the top of the hill, looked, and the young man was still there. He went to the bottom of the hill, looked and the young man was still there. He walked onto a beach and up to the waters edge, turned, and the young man was still there. He walked into the water up to his knees, turned, and he was still there. He walked until the water was to his waist, turned, and he was still there. He continued until the water was at his mid chest, turned, and now the water was near the young man's shoulders. Socrates quickly grabbed the young man by the shoulders and pushed him under the water and held him there! The young man started to squirm and twist! Then water bubbles started coming up from the water. Socrates then pulled the young man up out of the water and across his shoulder as he headed back toward the beach. He threw him down and gave him a couple breaths of air. The young man started to cough and breathe: he jumped up, reared back his fist and said, *"You crazy old fool! What are you trying to do? Kill me?"* Then Socrates raised his hand and said, *"Now wait I know you are mad, and you have the right to be; but let me ask you just one question."*

Young man: *"What is it?"*

Socrates: *"What was it that you wanted more than anything else in the world while I was holding you under the water?"*

Young man: *"Well, of course, I wanted a breath of air!"*

Socrates: *"when you desire success, as much as you desired that breath of air, that is when you will achieve it!"*

I hope my chapter on motivation has been of help and an inspiration to you. I know these stories and short sayings have helped me keep going when ever I have been discourage or the going got rough. It sometimes will for you as well, its like a test to see if you have what it takes, before the reward comes. The best of luck to you in your endeavor to be successful in your family, spiritual, and financial life.

One final tip: Make sure as you achieve different levels of success, to take time out to treat yourself and your family. Celebrate your achievements, and share it with your family, they are on your team, by fulfilling your life and making what you do possible!

CHAPTER 16

Case in Point # 1, Harlem Ave

I had been quite busy taking care of properties I already owned and following up on various leads. As will happen when you get real busy, some leads will simply not get followed up on. This was one of those leads. It was a property approaching the auction, located in the southwest suburb of Forestville. I kept meaning to drive by it. One day when I looked at my follow up file, I realized that this lead had just gone to the auction. I called the sheriff's department to find out what happened. This was also when there was a six-month redemption period after the auction. The bank was the successful bidder. I drove by that day. It was a nice brick bungalow with a two-car garage. The home was vacant. I was upset with myself for not following up sooner and buying at the auction for $1 over the bank's bid.

Now that the bank was the owner, perhaps I could make a deal with them. I talked with a neighbor who said the owner had moved very suddenly about four months earlier. She said she thought he was in trouble with the law. I decided to go inside to inspect the interior. I used my bolt cutters and cut the padlock off the hasp on the front door. "Is that legal?" You are probably thinking. It is a gray area at best. There is no one to complain. The owner is gone and not coming back. The bank is not the owner. Their only right at this point is to get the deed once the redemption period expires (this is when the redemption period took place after the auction) and to protect their collateral when it is believed to be abandoned. This is what they had done. Of course, I needed to see the inside to make a determination of what I might be able to do with the property. I replaced the padlock when I was done.

I was surprised at what I found. It did appear the owner had left in a hurry. He left some nice furniture including a big screen TV with an oak cabinet, a large sofa, recliner, china cabinet, dining room set, stove, refrigerator, washer, and dryer. These items would all belong to the new owner. In the floored walk up attic was nothing except a bed with two big movie camera type lights at the foot of the bed, pointed towards it. I will not bother speculating what that was about. In the two car garage was a truck that was in the process of being repainted. I knew the bank was the successful bidder at $45,000 on the first mortgage. I also knew that because it was vacant, I could plead for a shorter redemption period down to three months. I was confident the owner would not be coming back to redeem, or to get any of the personal items, I felt this was the case because of the length of time he had already been gone, because he was possibly in trouble with the law, and because of all the liens and total debt against the property. Therefore, I went back to my home office and called the bank. I asked for the person responsible for properties they foreclosed on and now own. After being switched around a few times, I reached the man responsible for the R.E.O.'s (Real Estate Owned). We will call him George. Our conversation went something like this:

Allen: Are you familiar with the address _____ S. Harlem Ave, Forestville?
George: Yes.
Allen: Is your mortgage a first? (Just to verify)
George: Yes.
Allen: Would you be willing to sell me the Certificate of Sale. (This is a document you get when being the successful bidder on a property. It entitles you to the deed at the expiration of the redemption period or judge's approval of sale.)
George: Yes, I would consider it for the right price.
Allen: Well, I know you have $45,000 into it. I will cash you out right now, and I will wait out the redemption period for the deed.
George: (He laughed.) Look, I know that home is worth $65,000. You will have to get a lot closer to that number in order for me to consider selling.
Allen: Well, what number would you consider accepting?
George: Oh, probably somewhere in the low $60's.
Allen: George, I would be buying it as an investor. I would lose money at that price.
George: That is your problem! I already have other interested parties at that price.
Allen: George, would you take my name and number in case the other parties do not come through for you?
George: No! You call me back when you are willing to pay the price.
  CLICK!

Talk about disappointment! Now I could really kick myself for not showing up at the auction. Occasionally you will come across bankers who do not seem very reasonable. However, I am no quitter! I went downtown and pulled the foreclosure case file. I found out who the other lien holders were against the property. These were junior liens to the first mortgage. There was a second and third mortgage, both with the same bank. The second was for $18,000, and the third was for $77,000. Well, these were obviously some cross-collateralized liens from some other debts the owner owed because my subject home was only worth $65,000. These liens were a big positive for me because as a junior lien, this bank had an interest in my subject property. They did not bid in at the auction above the first because that would have meant paying off the first, getting the

Allen Watkins

Certificate of Sale, and waiting out the redemption period. Apparently, either they were not interested, or they were not able to protect their interest. They had made the decision to allow their lien to be wiped out. However, just as the owner had a redemption period, so did the junior lien holders. As a junior lien holder, redeeming would mean having to republish, going to auction, and waiting out a six-month redemption period in order to get the deed. I was not really interested in going through all of that. However, maybe I could use the position as leverage with the banker George.

Looking further into the file, I found an interesting report. It was basically an interior inspection report written up by the security company that had drilled out the entry lock and installed the hasp and padlock. Apparently it was a report the bank was planning to use in going before the judge to get the redemption period reduced. The report stated that the home was vacant with only some garbage lying about. My interior inspection had certainly found it different! I guess George had some plans for all that personal property.

Back to my home office I went, where I called the bank with the second and third lien. They referred me to their attorney, Robert Levine (a fictitious name).

Allen: Robert Levine?
Robert: Yes.
Allen: Hi! My name is Allen Watkins. I understand you represent _____ Bank.
Robert: That is correct.
Allen: I am interested in purchasing your client's position or interest in the property at _____ S. Harlem Ave, Forestville. They have a second and third mortgage, and it appears they are just going to allow their interest to be wiped out since they did not bid in at the auction.
Robert: They could still redeem to protect their interest.
Allen: Yes, I understand that, but it seems unlikely because the value of the property is only $65,000 at best, it probably needs repairs and the first mortgage is owed $45,000.
Robert: What is it you are interested in doing?
Allen: I would like to give your client $2,000 and have them assign over their interest in the second and third mortgage.
Robert: I will call my client and get back to you.

Understand the importance of securing the interest of the third as well as the second was so that no one else could come in and buy out the third. I wanted complete control.

Robert called me back.

Robert: My client will not do it for $2,000 (My heart started to sink.), but they will do it for $2,500.

The Reality of Real Estate Investing

Yes! Yes! My adrenaline was flowing. The extra $500 was for his attorney fee, I am sure, but that was okay. I had just discounted an $18,000 second and a $77,000 third to $2,500.

I dialed George's number.

Allen: Hi, George! This is Allen Watkins. Remember me? I talked with you about buying the home at _____ S. Harlem Ave, Forestville.
George: Yes. You have reconsidered the price, have you?
Allen: No, Mr. Ambrose. In fact, I called to see if you would reconsider selling me your Certificate of Sale. You see, I just bought out the second and third mortgages, and now I have the right to pay you off; however, I would rather buy your Certificate of Sale.
George: (In a very angry tone) You did what? How dare you!
Allen: Mr. Ambrose, there is no need to get upset. This is just business. I'll pay the full $45,000 you have into the deal.
SILENCE...
George: Well, we have a little more into it than $45,000 that was not included in the court records. We spent $300 on insurance since we got the Certificate of Sale.
Allen: Okay. I will reimburse you for that. Will you be doing the paperwork through your attorney?

I was surprised at his initial angry response and relieved when he calmed down. Perhaps he was hoping to end up with the big screen TV. Oh well, that was that. Now I needed to put up money where my mouth was.

I contacted a private individual with whom I had already had conversations about investing with me. I informed him of the details about the property and the $47,800 total acquisition. I picked him up and showed him the property. We agreed he would be compensated 20% rate of return per annum, all due and payable upon the closing of the resale.

It was not really necessary to follow through with buying out the second and third mortgages since the first now was in agreement to sell. However, I had given my word. The deal closed. Immediately a For Sale sign went up. I called the local police about the truck in the garage. It turned out that it was stolen. They located the owner who came and picked it up. The police informed me the ex-owner was using the garage as a "chop shop," and the FBI was looking for him. That explains why he left so suddenly.

My attorney used the bank's inspection report and got the redemption period reduced to three months, with a credit of the time already passed. The home did need some cosmetic work, which I was anticipating doing. However, I got a buyer from the for sale sign right away, as is for $65,000. The deal closed within three months of the date I purchased it. After paying expenses and my investor his interest, I walked away with about $11,000 profit.

Case in Point # 2, Hoyne

I bought a brick bungalow located at 63rd and Hoyne, Chicago, at the auction. I paid around $20,000. I knocked on the door prior to the auction while doing my drive-by. The lady of the house told me that her situation was under control. When I pressed her for how she was solving her problem, she told me her attorney was taking care of it. This is a very common response. After I was the successful bidder at the auction, I knocked on her door to notify her that ownership had changed hands. Like most people, she invited me in at this point. We sat down and talked about the circumstances. She had divorced her husband about a year and a half ago. She worked full time, but on her income it was tough to make ends meet. She did not have any family or friends who would help her either. Her single twenty five year old daughter with two children and an eighteen year old son lived with her, neither of whom were bringing in any income. The housekeeping left much to be desired, and the basement was full of junk. Being a good-natured, caring person, I counseled her about her situation. I pointed out that she had been allowing her children to live off of her, which certainly contributed to her losing the home. I told her as long as she would pay some rent, cooperate with getting her daughter and son to get a job or public aid assistance, clean up the house, get her son to clean out the basement, the owner would allow her to stay for a couple months. This would help her get situated and give her time to find a new place to live. This would be like a new beginning for her and help the children to realize the seriousness of their situation and start showing some responsibility. She agreed to everything we talked about.

Well, she never paid a dime of the $400 rent we agreed upon (which was $200 below market rent), nor did they do anything else from what I could tell. I filed for eviction, and at my prompting she moved before the sheriff came out.

I spent about $10,000 fixing up the home. I added two bedrooms and a family room in the walk-up attic, and a bedroom in the basement. That gave me a total of six bedrooms, two on the second floor, three on the main level, and one in the basement. I rented the home to a husband and wife with nine children on the Section 8 program for $900 a month. They both worked, and they paid $68 rent plus the gas and electricity. Section 8 paid the rest each month. I paid the water which was required, or the tenant would have paid that, too. They were very strict with their children. When I would stop by occasionally, the children would be folding clothes or washing dishes. They kept a clean house. I refinanced the home for $35,000, paid off my investor, and had a positive cash flow of about $450 per month. About three years later I sold the house for $55,000.

What would have happened to the ex-owner if the bank had won the bid and got the house back as an R.E.O.? They would have evicted them quickly and swiftly with no questions asked. They would have had no communication with them. Therefore, to those of you whose first thought is,

"How can you take advantage of people when they are down and out?" I say, "It is simply a business opportunity that they have provided to me. If someone is going to profit from it, it might as well be me instead of the bank or another investor who may not approach them with the compassion that I do. The ex-owner was better off because I bought the property. It is just that simple."

Case in Point # 3, Forestville

A lady called me in response to one of the letters from my mailing. She was interested in getting help to keep her home. After our conversation I determined that she had a loan balance of around $10,000 on a home with a value of $45,000 to $50,000. Since this certainly was a good candidate for a sale - lease back agreement, I made an appointment.

The home was a raised ranch, three bedroom, one and a half bath with a one - car attached garage and a fenced rear yard. It was in average condition but needed a new roof. She was working full time as a nurse and had her sister living with her. She explained that her husband was abusive, but they were now divorced. He had caused her much financial trouble. She wanted to keep the home. I described to her my plan of the "Sale / Lease Back with Option" as explained in Chapter Five. She said she needed to think about it. As I pressed, I determined that her ex-husband was still on the title. She assured me she could get him to sign off.

I followed up with her in a couple of days. She said she was checking into other possibilities but I should call her back in a couple of weeks. I did and got the same response. I started checking with her each month until eventually I saw her property appear on the sheriff's sale list. I informed her and still she claimed to be checking into other financing possibilities.

I went to the auction and won the bid for a dollar more at $14,424. As soon as the auction was over, a man approached me and asked if that was the final sale for the property. I told him, "Yes." Later I figured that he must have been her ex-husband.

I had brought $2,000 deposit money with me. Now I rushed over to the bank and took out cash advances on my credit cards. I went back to the sheriff's office and paid for the property in full.

I went back to the property and informed the lady that I was now managing the property for the investor who had bought it at the auction. She asked about being able to still work something out to keep the property. I told her it was too late to save her equity. The investor I worked for was now the new owner.

She then asked if she could at least rent the house. I asked why she would want to do that when she would have to pay more in rent than her mortgage had been. She stated the obvious — she would have to pay rent somewhere anyway. It wasn't that she could not afford it; it was because of her dispute with her ex-husband that she did not make the payments to start with, and she would really like to not give him the satisfaction of knowing she had to move.

I verified her job and income and entered into a lease for $550 a month. I could have evicted her and rented the home and got $650 or $700 a month rent. However, the deal before me would work, so why get greedy. I refinanced the home with a new first mortgage for $29,000 — P.I.T.I. for $349 a month. I paid off my credit cards and the other expenses within three months. I put just over $13,000 profit in my pocket tax-free because it was borrowed money.

Case in Point # 4, Burbank

I got a call from a man who said he had gotten my letter and was interested in selling his home. He owed around $30,000 and wanted an offer. I knew the location was good. Of course I made an appointment with him right away. When I arrived at the home, I got no answer. I waited fifteen minutes and then left a note. Later I called; no answer. I stopped by the property again one day. A woman answered the door. She said, "My husband is not home. You will have to talk with him." She abruptly shut the door. I knocked again, and she would not answer.

I attempted a contact a couple of more times over the next several months. No response. The address appeared on the auction list. My desire was to make a deal with the owners prior to the auction to avoid competition. I knocked on the door again. The woman answered the door. I immediately explained that I was not trying to bother her, but the property was scheduled for auction. I would hate to see her get nothing when I could possibly get her some money if she would talk with me. She asked, "How much?" I told her it all depended on the condition of the property. I asked her, "Would you allow me to inspect the interior? It will only take a minute." She did allow me to walk through. I learned the reason I never saw her husband; they were separated and getting a divorce. She did verify for me that her ex-husband would be available for a signature.

The home needed much work. There were only two bedrooms; the tiny kitchen needed to be gutted and a wall taken down to open it up to make it larger. I told her I would consult with my investor and get back with her.

I figured about $15,000 was needed to fix the home up right. I would be borrowing the money from an armchair investor by paying a $1,000 origination fee and 20% interest per annum, due and payable upon my re-sell. The numbers were getting tight. I felt I could only offer her $1,000. She said she would talk with her ex-husband and get back to me. She would not return my calls. Therefore, I went to the auction and won the bid for a dollar more at $34,026. I was delighted that there was no competition.

The ex-owner moved right away on her own, refusing to respond to my attempts to communicate with her. As the remodeling was nearing completion, I got a buyer for the full price at $69,900. After the real estate commission and expenses, I netted about $17,000.

Case in Point # 5, Barry

I was looking through the list of properties approaching the auction one day and came across the address 1255 W. Barry in the Lake View area of Chicago. I knew the location was a good one. The judgment amount was about $2,300. The plaintiff was the City of Chicago. This information indicated to me that the city was foreclosing on a demolition lien. Although I was not familiar with the values, I figured the lot had to be worth at a minimum $30,000.

On the drive by, the lot was not particularly impressive. It was an overgrown corner lot (25' x 125') with some debris. What was impressive was the area. There was great evidence of development taking place. I decided it was worth further investigation. I went downtown to research the court file. I learned that just over five years earlier a Michael L. bought a five-unit building on the lot from a David J. on contract. He signed a mortgage note for $21,000. Apparently Michael let the building deteriorate until the city tore it down.

I set out to locate the owner Michael. I came up with three different addresses; however, he had moved from each one. I felt I was at a dead end trying to locate him.

Then I decided to see if I could locate David J. I went to the phone book. There were about twenty five names. Half-way through the list I found the right person. I verified that he was the holder of the note. I mentioned that it looked like he did not come out of his deal with Michael L. very well. He said, "Yea, he never made a single payment and ran the building down."

I said, "Yes, and the city tore it down and is now foreclosing on the lot. It looks like you are about to get wiped out."

"Yea,"" he said. "I had an attorney pursuing it, but it has been five years, and he has not been able to do anything; so I guess I'll just let it go."

I said, "Well, would you consider signing over your mortgage note to me to see if I can do anything with it?"

He said, "For nothing?"

"Well, I would be taking a chance because we do not know for sure if I will be able to do anything or not."

He said, "It would not be worth my time to meet with you."

I said, "What would be worth your time?"

He said, "Fifty dollars."

I said, "OK, I will risk fifty dollars; do you know of a notary close by?"

He said, "Yes, at the Currency Exchange around the corner."

"Great, I can be there in an hour. Oh, by the way, I just noticed that your wife is also on the note. Will she also be available to sign the paper work?"

"Well, OK, if it doesn't take long," he said.

I called my attorney immediately to ask what paper work I needed to do to have the owners of a note sign over their interest to me. It was a simple letter of assignment. I got it together and picked up David J. and his wife, They lived in a newer town home in the desirable Lincoln Park area of Chicago. He mentioned to me that he owned several properties and that he had just made a mistake with this one. We went to the nearest Currency Exchange. They signed, it was notarized, and I gave them the fifty dollars. My impression was that they thought I had just bought something that had no value. I was very hopeful that I was not wasting my time or money.

I was by no means a seasoned investor at that point. In fact, I would say I was still green. However, I felt good about what I had just done. Now I needed a partner because I had no money. I knew I had to hire an attorney to file foreclosure on my note. That would be $2,000 to $3,000. I had to pay off the city of Chicago $2,300 for their demolition lien, and there was another couple thousand in back taxes.

The next night I got a call from David J. He told me that he had gotten a call from an attorney also interested in buying the note from him. He said, *"Maybe you tricked me and I should not have signed over my note to you. I want you to give it back."*

I responded, "I did not trick you or do anything dishonest."

He said, *"Well, how about we get together and talk about it before I have to get my attorney involved?"* I told him I would have to consult with my partner and get back with him. I did, and we agreed that I should talk to him. When I met with him and his wife, he basically repeated himself, and I did the same. I pointed out that they thought they were selling me nothing. I only knew I was sticking my neck out for fifty dollars and hoping I would be able to do something to make a profit. We left it at that point and said we would both give it some thought. I never heard from him again.

I offered a 50% partnership to my attorney, since she advised me on how to secure the note in the first place. She paid off the demolition fee and back taxes, and we hired a foreclosure attorney. About two and a half months later the foreclosure attorney received a request for a pay-off letter on my note from an attorney representing Michael L. Apparently still as the owner, he entered into a contract to sell the lot to a developer for $105,000, who planned to build a row of town homes.

Remember, the face value of my note was $21,000, and no payments had been made for five years. After calculating all the back interest and cost we had into it protecting our mortgage note, a check was cut to me at the closing for

$49,500. Minus the $6,000 my partner had put out in expenses. We were left with $42,500 to split.

All of this took place within three months. It was not bad for a guy who did not know much but was willing to risk a little and put forth the effort to make it happen.

Case in Point # 6, Hickory Hills

I had been driving by properties all day. Thus far none had excited me. However, when I drove by the 9200 block of 86th Place in Hickory Hills, I became excited. It was a large, split-level in a very nice area of custom-built homes. The foreclosure judgment was about $60,000 and value over $100,000.

There was no answer at the door. I left a note and went to talk with the neighbor. He told me the owners had moved. He also told me that the owner worked at R. R. Donnelly. I thanked him and went back to the house and started walking around. Knowing that it was vacant and the auction was soon approaching, I wanted to know what the interior condition was like. The only source of entry I found was a rear open window on the upper level. I stood on a garbage can and was able to reach the window and get inside.

Daring, you may be thinking; wrong, you may be thinking. Well, I suppose it depends on your perspective. Legally there has to be someone to complain or press charges. I have only had the police called on me once. (See Case in Point # 7, Streamwood.) The owner has abandoned the property, and the bank is not yet the owner. Although lenders do have the right to secure and protect their interest in abandoned property, generally they do not know they are vacant, as in this case.

I know my activity is not with malicious intent. In fact, any activity I am involved with is for a positive effect — whether it is for the owner, the bank, or both, as well as for myself. This you will come to understand as the story unfolds. If at all possible, I have to know what the interior condition is to make the best possible decision.

I found that there were four large bedrooms, two and a half baths, a huge living room with a double-sided stone fireplace, a large kitchen with a dining area, a large recreation room, and an unfinished sub-basement. The interior needed some general remodeling. The kitchen cabinets were quality wood but needed refinishing. A new kitchen floor was needed as well as carpeting and painting throughout. The family bathroom needed to be finished with ceramic tile on the wall around the tub, plus a few other things. Now I had a good idea of what I was dealing with.

Confident with the information I already had, and confirmed by the attorney's office, I went to the auction a little early so that I could have a chance to look over the court file. When I attempted to check it out, the clerk informed me that it was already checked out. "Guess I will be having competition," I thought. I looked around at the people sitting at the table going through files and recognized one man as a person who taught Real Estate seminars and acclaimed himself to be wealthy from real estate investments. As I looked closer, sure enough, he was looking at the file that belonged to the Hickory Hills house.

I became worried. I knew I was willing to go up to $85,000, but I did not want to. Perhaps a deeper pocket like his would be willing to pay more. I, of course, did not have a deep pocket; I was getting the money from an investor and paying a $1,000 origination fee and 20% per annum, all due and payable upon a re-finance or re-sell. Another factor was that this property fell under the old law where the six-month redemption period took place after the auction; therefore, there was no deed for six months. However, I knew when the property was vacant, I could get the court to reduce it to three months. I was figuring the home was worth about $125,000 to $130,000 and needed about $15,000 worth of work. I was also thinking it had potential as a personal residence.

Anyhow, I was feeling that my chances for a successful bid were slim. The bidding started out at a little over $64,000. I quickly jumped in and said a dollar more. My competitor bid $65,000; I bid $66,000. On we went until he bid $70,000, and I jumped the bid to $74,000. He did not bid any more. The sheriff said, "Once, twice," and then another investor who was a regular who had been buying at the auction for years bid $74,100. My heart sank; another deep pocket! I bid $75,000. He bid $75,100. I bid $79,000, and there was silence. The sheriff said, "Once, twice, thrice, sold." I had won! I was delighted!

Later I began to wonder why my competition was not willing to pay more. Then I realized that they did not have the advantage of a description of what the interior was like. Now I had the redemption period to contend with. Since some serious bidding had taken place, there was a surplus of money available to the owner which amounted to about $14,000. All he had to do was have an attorney go in and petition the court for the money. However, most of the time the ex-owners of foreclosures are not even aware of this and never collect. Well, I had an incentive to contact the ex-owner. If I could buy his redemption rights, then I would be able to go ahead and get the deed to the home and not have to wait out the redemption period.

When I called his place of employment, they said they did not put through personal calls, but they did tell me he worked the midnight shift. Trying to contact him at work seemed to be my only option since there was no forwarding address from his previous residence.

Therefore, I went to the R R Donnelly plant at 11:30 P.M. There was a guarded check-in entrance for the employees. I talked with the guards. They had a list of everyone due into work that night. I asked them to check on my owner; I will refer to him as Mr. Smith. They informed me that he was not scheduled to work that night but was scheduled for the next night.

I returned the next night and kept asking men as they approached the entrance, "Are you Mr. Smith?" until no more were coming. When I inquired of the guards, they made a phone call and found that he had called in sick. I returned the following night and finally got to talk with him. He was a little hesitant and in a hurry to get to work. I basically said, "I am sure you are aware, your property in Hickory Hills went to auction. I work for the investor who was the successful bidder. I do not know if you are aware of it or not, but there is some money available for you."

He interrupted and asked, "How much?"

I replied, "About $14,000, and since it appears you are not planning to redeem the property, my investor would like to offer to buy your redemption rights by paying for an attorney to get the $14,000 released to you from the courts."

He said, "I will have to think about it." I got his home phone number and agreed to give him a day to think about it; then I would give him a call. When I did, he agreed and proceeded to explain to me why he lost the home. His wife had medical problems that were costing him a large amount. He had two children in college, and he was paying for everything. He did some complaining, and I just listened, which is what some people need you to do. I felt from his comments that the children were the biggest problem — spoiled brats. He was making $40,000 a year. It seemed to me the children were taking advantage and dad was letting them — to the point of causing him serious loss. This was not the first time, I had seen this scenario.

The deal was made. I put about $15,000 into repairs and moved in. I got an appraisal that came in at $120,000. Since I did not like that, I got another one that came in at $155,000 and I refinanced it for a $120,000 first mortgage. I lived there for about two and a half years and then sold it for $160,000.

The interesting thing about that sale was that I first tried to sell it "by owner" for a couple of months at $149,900 and got a couple of low ball offers. Then I listed it with a Realtor for $162,000 at a 6% commission. I got a $160,000 offer in two weeks and netted at the closing $150,400. That is the power of the M.L.S.

Now back to the issue of whether I did wrong by entering the home. Let us look at what resulted. The bank was paid off, but they would have been, regardless. The owner got $14,000 as a result of my knowing what the interior was like which allowed me to bid as much as I did. If another investor had won the bid, he may not have attempted to contact the owner. The owner may have never known about the surplus, or it would not have been as much. Or, the other investor may have charged him a percentage to help him get the money.

It is a personal judgment call.

Case in Point # 7, Streamwood

This was my very first deal. It was a management deal. I had mailed many letters. Then I got a phone call from a lady who had gotten one of my letters. She wanted to know what, if anything, I could do for her. While talking with her, she told me she and her husband were going through a divorce. He had moved out, and then she moved out. After questioning her, I determined that the home was over indebted. She told me it needed a lot of work. I explained, based on the amount of work she described, the most I could offer her would be to manage it during the foreclosure process. That way it would not just continue to deteriorate, with the bank eventually getting much less money for it, and possibly going after her and her husband for a deficiency judgment. I went on to say I would invest the time and money in putting the property in rentable condition. Then I would try to get my money back and compensation for my time by renting the property out until the bank completed the foreclosure. The bank, of course, would be able to sell the property for more money because of its improved condition. Then there was silence. Finally she said, *"Well, I guess you will need to go look at it."*

I replied, *"Yes, how can I get the keys?"*

She said, *"There aren't any; I lost them."* Then she went on to tell me that I could probably get in through the bathroom window at the back of the house. I said, *"OK, if that is the only way I can get in."*

I was hopeful and yet doubtful that I would really be able to take care of all the work she described. I went prepared with an entry lock and a "For Rent" sign. I parked in the driveway and was able to get in through the window as she said. It did need much work. However, I was excited with the opportunity to do my first rental deal. I thought I would at least give it a try. I would not do any work until I got the first and last month's rent first, I thought.

While I was changing the lock, the police pulled up.

They asked me what I was doing. I explained *"Inspecting the property condition, and now I am changing the lock."*

One of the policemen then said, *"A neighbor reported you broke in through the bathroom window."* I then explained the whole story about the house being in foreclosure, the owner called me, etc. They looked around inside the house and then left. I knew from that point on I would need to talk to the neighbors first.

I finished installing the lock, put up the for rent sign and left. Later I got a call from a single guy inquiring about it. He was a construction worker. He was excited about doing the work in exchange for the first and last month's rent and a reduced monthly rent. The monthly rental for the area was $700. I rented it to him for $500. I did not spend a dime. I did require that he give me the second month's rent up front. I collected rent from him for about fourteen months. When I was notified that the bank was the owner, I turned it over to them.

Case in Point # 8, Rockwell

One day while driving by properties, I came across a brick three - unit with a full basement and two car garage. It looked very interesting, specifically because I was looking at a balance of around $6,000 with the auction coming up in about two weeks.

The first floor tenant turned out to be the daughter of the owner. Her dad, who had been divorced, had died. Apparently there were some complicated family problems. Anyhow, she was poorly managing the building and not taking care of repairs. The second and third floor apartments were also occupied, but the occupants were not paying rent. She was actually in distress about her situation, feeling a great amount of pressure, and talking on and on. She was also behind in the utilities for the building. She was very cooperative with information about the building and in showing me through it. The tenants as well were very cooperative. They, of course, were hopeful for a new owner who would take care of the building. It needed around $10,000 in repairs. I figured it was worth about $60,000 to $70,000.

Of course with such a low mortgage balance, competition could be very stiff. The problem, however, was that no estate had been opened, and there could be other family members who might be heirs. (Going through the auction would clean the title up.) Trying to deal with potential heirs and the legal issues of getting an estate organized enough to sell the property would just be a nightmare.

Therefore, I decided it would be best to just take my chances at the auction and hope for the best. The daughter of the owner on the first floor did not care what I did as long as I would pay her past - due utility bills to make them current. That was around $500. Since I was still in my early years in the business, I did not have the money myself, I lined up another investor who was also an attorney. It was easy convincing him it was a good investment with an easy $50,000 as security. His compensation for providing the acquisition money was $1,000 origination fee and 20% per annum, all due and payable upon the sale or refinance.

To the auction we went. Since this was the first time this young attorney ever made an investment of this kind, he wanted to be a part the excitement of the auction. I even had him do the bidding. That was nice of me! We were concerned about competition and the auction price being bid up or being out - bid. We were only prepared to bid to $20,000. When the sheriff announced the bid, my investor quickly bid $1 more as I had instructed him. He did a superb job. Ever hear the term "Silence is Golden?" Then the sheriff said, "Once, twice, trice, sold!" I was ecstatic! We instructed the sheriff to prepare the certificate of sale in my name, and I signed a mortgage note with my investor.

The next day I got a phone call from an investor who congratulated me on my successful bid. He went on to tell me that he had planned to bid at the auction, also, but had gotten there late. Then he offered me $20,000 to sell him the certificate of sale. I was tempted; however, I resisted.

I told the daughter on the first floor that I would pay off her utilities, but I needed her to move first. She agreed. The tenant on the second floor had already made plans to move. The third floor tenant wanted to stay and would actually be an asset as the building manager and janitor for $50 a month reduced rent. That worked out well.

I did the necessary repair work, applied for a refinance, and got a mortgage for $46,000 within about three months. That represented a considerable amount of profit after paying back all the expenses. The kicker was that the profit was "Tax Free" because it was borrowed money. Then I got an energy conservation loan for $10,000. I put in new separate heat systems and hot water heaters for each apartment, and updated the electricity.

About seven years later I sold the building for, now brace yourself $125,000.

Case in Point # 9, Foster Avenue

I drove by a two unit grey stone building. A nice Hispanic family lived there. It was obvious to me that I was talking to the Mom and Dad. However, we were not communicating very well because they spoke no English and I spoke no Spanish. As I was about to leave, their teenage daughter arrived home from school. She spoke English. They were tenants, and other tenants lived on the second floor. I explained about the building being in foreclosure, but not to worry; perhaps they could stay on as tenants for awhile. However, it was certain they would have to move in a couple of months if I could make a deal. The building would need about $30,000 of rehab work. It was still interesting because I was looking at a mortgage balance of about $12,000. After rehab the building would be worth over $100,000.

I found out from the tenant that the owner's husband had died. He had left the wife with a large debt. She had filed a bankruptcy and moved back to Mexico. They had not heard any more from her, and it had been over six months.

Well, I certainly had some research to do. I went downtown to investigate the court file. I learned that there was a second mortgage for about $28,000 and several smaller liens totaling over $90,000. I thought that was good because less aggressive investors would think "over-indebted" and move on. However, I knew there was more research to be done. I contacted the first mortgage attorney and asked if his client might be interested in selling his mortgage. He agreed to ask him and get back to me. I contacted the second mortgage attorney who had filed an appearance in the first mortgage foreclosure proceedings. The first thing I asked was whether his client was planning to bid in at the auction. He told me yes. I asked if his client would consider selling the mortgage. He thought he would, but only for full value. I determined that none of the other liens planned on representing themselves. So here are the facts I had to deal with.

- Owners: Husband died. Wife is left with a property that needs much work and that is overburdened with debt. She filed bankruptcy and moved to Mexico. She has not been heard from in six months.
- Liens on the property: First and second clearly intend to protect their interest. This means the second would be paying off the first. Total of both liens about $40,000.
- All the other liens would be wiped out.
- About $40,000 in rehab and miscellaneous cost.
- Could be put on the market for $139,900 and probably sell at $135,000.
- That left $55,000 in potential profit.

It was definitely worth pursuing. I decided to buy the mortgages. I did not have to worry about the owner returning to try and save the property or filing bankruptcy while I was foreclosing on the mortgages because she had already filed.

I worked out a deal of 50% of the net proceeds with an investor whose full time job was as a Chicago Police Officer. I bought the first and second mortgages for full value. I kept the same foreclosing attorneys. The auction was only about a month away. At the auction if another investor bid, I certainly would bid it up, In the "worst case scenario" I would get all the money back. However, no one bid, and I got it because I owned the mortgage notes. A couple months later I sold it for $132,000 without a realtor commission.

Case in Point # 10, West Chicago

I received a letter back stamped "MLNA" (moved, left no address) by the post office. I drove by the property and found it vacant. I called the attorney representing the bank in the foreclosure to check on the balance owed and if a first or second mortgage was being foreclosed. He inquired if I was interested in buying the property. I told him possibly. He went on to say that he had gotten a phone call from the owner the day before and gave me his name and number. Now, that was a helpful attorney! I had already determined that the debt was too close to the value. In my discussion with the owner, he agreed with that fact. So I worked out a management agreement with him for 50/50 split of the rental income after all expenses. The home was basically in move-in condition except for the water pipes that had burst in the winter cold. Fortunately there was easy access to the breaks, and they were reasonable to repair. I rented the home for $500 a month. It lasted about 10 months; then the bank took over.

Case in Point #11, Summit

I got a call from someone who just wanted to tell me that the person I had sent my letter to was dead. Of course, I could not just leave it at that. I inquired who the caller was. The reply was, "A tenant" I pressed on and found out this was a three-unit building. Since the owner died, his sister was managing the building. She lived forty five minutes away and was not taking care of repairs in the building. I asked for the sister's name and number. When I called, she confirmed what I had been told and added two more details that had been left out by the tenant.

1. Tenants were not paying rent, and that was why repairs were not being done.
2. Two of the tenants were her cousins, and they had been disputing ever since her brother died. I immediately thought, "Opportunity." I suggested that perhaps an outside party from the family, a property manager such as myself, might be able to get control of the property and get cooperation from the tenants. I worked out a management agreement with her for a 50/50 split of the rental income after all expenses.

I contacted each of the tenants in person with an official looking letter. The letter head contained my management company information, and the letter notified them of the new management and the due date of the rent. I also gave them each a five-day notice for the rent. (That is first step of the eviction process.) It let them know I was serious about the business at hand. I asked the tenants what repairs they were aware of that were needed. I made a list and assured them repairs would be done as long as they paid their rent. Two tenants stayed and paid; one moved.

The debt was approximately what it was worth "as is."

The rental income was $450 for two of the units and $300.00 for the third. It cost about $500 for the minimal repairs.

At about ten months into it, just a couple weeks before the foreclosure auction, I asked the sister to call the attorneys for the lender and ask for a payoff letter. I wanted to see exactly where the numbers were because I had someone interested in buying. As it turned out the debt was a little too much to make a deal. Since it was an FHA mortgage, there could be no discounting. To my surprise, when this property came up for the auction, it was cancelled.

Apparently a clerk, paralegal, or perhaps even an attorney made a mistake and cancelled the auction because of the request for a payoff letter. I could not believe it! It was not just a postponement, but a cancellation. They had to start the foreclosure process all over. We had the property for almost another year.

Case in Point # 12, Evergreen Park

I came across an address in the Foreclosure Directory. The balance was about $27,000. I knew the area was quite nice and had much more value than that. I tried Information for the owner's phone number. It was not listed. I decided to try calling the neighbors. I used the criss-cross directory and started calling. The neighbor told me it was a nice brick home and that an older lady lived there by herself. Her husband had died about a year earlier. She was a recluse and was believed to be an alcoholic.

In considering the situation and a strategy for my approach, I decided upon the following: My wife's mother was in town visiting, she was probably about the same age as this woman. I asked my wife and mother-in-law to knock on the door while I waited in the car. A few minutes later they waved for me to come on in. It worked! They got my foot in the door.

She had a couple layers of clothes on and a sweater.

The curtains were drawn shut with minimal lights on. She told us several people had been knocking on the door, but she would just slam it in their face. She was really very friendly. She told us how she had cared for her husband for a year and a half and that he had died about a year earlier. She was aware of what was happening, but she was just lacking any motivation or energy to do anything about it. She had no plan nor intentions to develop a plan. She was an educated woman who seemed to be in a state of depression.

After discussing the circumstances and making sure she understood what was going on and what needed to happen, I suggested that she allow me to sell the home for her and earn a realtor commission. She owed about $30,000. I would sell it for $85,000 - a quick-sale price. My commission would be $5,000, and she would net around $48,000 after the closing costs. I asked if this was what she wanted to do to move forward and solve her problem. It became obvious that she could not make a decision. I finally said, "Tell you what; I can see you are having a hard time making a decision. So I am going to go ahead and write up an agreement for me to sell your home. Otherwise, I am afraid you are going to end up out in the street!" I wrote it up, and with some encouragement she signed it.

Although I had a real estate license, my focus was normally investing, not brokering. Therefore, I was not a member of the M.L.S. I had my sales license with an attorney who also had his broker's license. (A sales license can only operate under a broker's license) This was so my license would remain active and not be terminated by the state. Our agreement was that I would give him 10% of any commissions I earned.

I counseled the owner about showing the home and getting ready to move once it sold. I was concerned about her lack of motivation. Her home was full and cluttered.

I ran an ad in the local newspaper and as luck would have it, I got a buyer right away for the full price! I counseled with the owner about preparing to move. She needed to be packing, finding a place to rent, renting a truck, and so on. As the closing date approached it became apparent she lacked the ability to do anything for herself. Thus, I lined up an apartment for her and hired people to help with the packing and moving. Then we closed the sale. She netted just under $50,000.

Case in Point # 13, 76 Unit

In all fairness I need to admit right up front that I did not personally negotiate this deal; my mentor did. He was approached by a lender who had heard of him from another lender with whom he had done business. There was a 76 unit building in the Hyde Park area in the southern part of Chicago. This is an affluent area of Chicago's south side. The subject property was run-down and mismanaged; it was about half occupied and half of those were undesireables. However, it had potential! The debt on it was $1.2 million. The acquisition price was negotiated down to $700,000. A rehab loan was provided for one million dollars and a one year moratorium, which means forgiveness of any payments or interest.

I took over the management and hired a secretary, building engineer, and janitor. I took control of the tenants and got rid of the undesireables. I kept the building rented as much as possible. I moved tenants around as was necessary during the remodeling. The income I collected was what I used to operate the building and pay myself a salary of $1000 a month. Although running the building took a great amount of time, it was a good experience and still allowed me time to make other deals.

We finished the rehabilitation and sold the building eleven months later for two million dollars. All of this was done just one month before the first mortgage payment became due.

Case in Point # 14, Natchez

I received an assignment from one of my lender clients near Midway Airport in Chicago. It was a bungalow with a full basement. I gave the client my suggested list price of $99,900 as is and $109,900 repaired. This particular client always got his own appraisal, also. Instead of coming in high, as I was used to, the appraiser came in low. To my surprise, the client authorized me to put the home on the market for $79,900. We sold it immediately to one of my investors for $77,000. With some repairs he sold it himself for $105,000. You just never know!

Case in Point # 15, Dickens

I found an address in the directory that was approaching the auction. It was a five unit building, all brick, in the Bucktown area of Chicago. The owner lived in the building, and it was fully rented. It soon became apparent from the smell and his demeanor that the owner was drunk. He denied the foreclosure. I returned three or four times, getting more information from the tenants than the owner. I tried to get through to the owner, to make a deal and avoid competition at the auction. However, the owner was an alcoholic and could not be reasoned with. The debt was about $40,000. I bought it at the auction for a dollar more.

Since I still could not reason with the owner, he had to be evicted. We had to repair a broken sewer line, and then we sold the building right away for $85,000.

Case in Point # 16, 96th Place

I drove by this property on Chicago's southeast side one day while driving by several leads. It was an all brick two story duplex. Each unit was independently owned. It was approaching the auction in a couple days for about $14,000.

I knocked on the door. An older lady answered and informed me that her daughter owned the unit and that she was renting from her daughter under the Section 8 program. I called the daughter and she quickly informed me that it was all taken care of.

I called and verified the property was still scheduled the morning of the auction, and it was. I went and won the bid for a dollar more. I left the auction, walked a couple blocks to a bank, took out cash advances on my credit cards enough to pay for the property. I then immediately went and informed the lady in the unit that ownership had change hands. I told her I would like to keep her on as a tenant. She gave me the name and number of her Section 8 representive, and

Allen Watkins

I toured the unit. It had two bedrooms, a dining room, full unfinished basement, and a two car garage, and was in good condition. All that was left for me to do was take a copy of my Sheriff's Deed to Section 8, and they started sending me the monthly rent of $475. With-in three months I had refinanced the town home with a first mortgage for $30,000. The appraisal came in at $45,000. I paid off the credit cards and put about $15,000 in my pocket. It was tax free, because it was borrowed money. I had a positive cash flow of about $50. Now that is the kind of "No Money Down" deals I like to do! It was no money out of my own pocket and $15,000 tax free into my pocket.

I had noticed before that the unit next door sharing a wall with my unit was vacant. However, now I had a more keen interest. I started looking into the windows and saw there was work to be done on the interior. The side door was unlocked, and I was able to inspect the interior more closely. I became excited because it was clear that whoever owned it had a problem they could not keep up with. I also knew if I could acquire ownership of this unit, I would then control the whole building. This unit also had a third bedroom addition and no garage.

The first thing I did was to check if it was in foreclosure in the chancery department of the court house where I pulled the foreclosure files. It was! I checked the summons and found the address the owner was served at, just a few miles from the subject. I also learned that the first mortgage balance was in the teens. However, there was a second mortgage for about $15,000. After four attempts of leaving notes on the door at the address I got a phone call. The woman had been through a divorce. She was interested in selling and swore the second mortgage had been paid off. However, she was never able to produce a "Release of Lien" document to prove it. Because the lien holder was out of business, she could not prove it through them. Apparently they just never recorded the Release of Lien when it was paid off. Therefore, it remained on the title and would only be cleared through the foreclosure process.

Since there had been no competition with the other unit that was in good condition and it had no second mortgage, I was hopeful there would be no competition for this unit, also. There was competition though, but I won the bid at $15,400. I remodeled the unit for about $10,000 and rented it through section 8, also. I refinanced it for about $30,000. The appraisal came in at $47,000.

Case in Point # 17, Harvey

I received an assignment from one of my lender clients on a split-level home. It was vacant and in need of rehab. I performed my inspection and market analysis and turned in my reports. I recommended $24,900 as a list price. It needed about $15,000 in repairs and had a repaired value of $55,000 to $60,000.

I received a buyer referral from one of the loan officers with whom I did business. The buyer was already approved for financing. Her area, price range, and desired home features all matched this house in repaired condition. I showed it to her and helped her visualize what it would look like when it was remodeled. She saw the vision and was excited.

I put together a deal with an investor to buy the home, remodeled it then close on a sale to my buyer. He closed on his purchase, got the work done and closed with my buyer all within thirty days. He netted about $19,000.

Case in Point # 18, DesPlaines

A lead I was following up on turned out to be a town home. The neighbor informed me that the owner had died. In the court file there was an attorney who had opened the estate and was acting as the executor. There was one heir living in South Carolina. The attorney was not sure what the heir intended to do. However, he was conducting an Estate Sale for all the furniture in the home. I attended and found the home in decent condition. It just needed a fresh paint job and a new carpet.

The balance on the mortgage was about $32,000, and the value was $70,000. Why the attorney / executor did not put the home on the market was a mystery. It did go to auction, and I did win the bid for a dollar more. However, I divided the pie three ways. I was using my mentor as a financial partner. At the auction I met up with an investor I knew who was also there to bid on this property. We agreed to split the deal three ways unless someone else was also there bidding. In that case, we would each be on our own. We got it for a dollar more, spent less than $5,000 on it and sold it for $70,000 through a realtor.

Case in Point #19, Mohawk

This occurred when I was still working towards my first ownership deal. I had a few management deals already under my belt. The property looked like a two-unit with a full basement. When there was no answer at the door, I left a note.

There was around $50,000 owed; depending on the condition, this could be borderline for investing in. However, this area of Chicago was the Logan Square neighborhood, and it was experiencing significant appreciation at the time. I also thought this might be a consideration for a personal residence.

I left a note on three more occasions. Still I received no call. I decided that was not working, and I needed to do something different. I changed the wording on my note and wrote, "Sorry to keep bothering you; however, my wife will not let me give up until I hear from you. Please help!" It worked! The owner told me that statement was the reason he finally called.

The building was vacant with two units. The first floor needed too much work to do anything about it now. The second floor needed a fresh paint job and some minor repairs. The basement had an illegal make-shift apartment.

We worked out a lease option. I gave the owner $500 for possession, and another $500 would be due when I was able to work out a deal with the bank for a short payoff. While I was getting the two apartments ready to rent, I was approached by a young guy who had heard about the basement apartment from the previous tenant. I told him it was not in good enough condition. He said he would fix it up himself and pay me $200 a month for rent. I could not turn down easy money like that. I put about $600 into the second floor apartment and rented it for $550 a month.

I did make the bank an offer for $55,000; however, they kept stringing me along for about six months until they got the deed. Then they sold it to someone else for $62,000. Perhaps I tried to negotiate too good of a deal for myself. Anyway, I still made out with the rents I had collected.

Case in Point # 20, Wentworth

I became excited as soon as I drove by this lead. There was two houses on a corner lot. One was a large two-story frame on the rear, and a one-story brick home was on the front of the lot. A nice looking large church was across the street, and an elementary school was across the other street diagonally.

There was no answer at either door. While I was walking around the property, a young adult male approached me and asked who I was looking for. I explained I was looking for the owner. He said his uncle was in jail. If I had any questions, I could talk with his grandmother who lived a couple houses over. After talking with me, she agreed to allow the young man to show me through the homes.

However, I would have to call her daughter about trying to buy the houses from the owner, her son. The daughter kept in contact with her brother while he was in jail.

The time for the auction was soon approaching. The opening bid would be around $13,000. I figured it was worth about $60,000, and it would be more with some remodeling. The rear home had three bedrooms, a large living room, an eat-in kitchen, and a full bath on the first floor. The second floor had the same square footage. It was all open, like a large party room with a wet bar, full bath, and a bedroom. My idea was to make another bedroom with some of that space. In addition the home had a full unfinished basement. The front home had a large living room, kitchen, dining room, and one bedroom. My plan was to keep it for the rental value.

The sister was a pretty tough negotiator. I offered $20,000, but she would not budge off of $30,000. I finally agreed, and she got the brother's signature in jail. I ended up having to give the attorneys for the bank $5,000 as earnest money toward paying off the mortgage to postpone the auction. That allowed my attorney time to examine the title and prepare for closing.

I went to the auction to bid on another property on the same date that this one was scheduled for. The commissioner, as it happened to be in this case, of course announced it had been cancelled. There were two other investors there to bid on it. I, of course, had already gotten it.

I rented the rear home for $900 a month and the front home for $400. It has been a great cash flow ever since.

Case in Point # 21, Avers

I came across a three-unit greystone, I really like these buildings. It was going to the auction for about $20,000. I knocked on the first floor door. It was a tenant who said the owner lived on the second floor. He was a nice enough guy; however, he was an obvious drunk, sixty something years old. He acted as if the foreclosure was all taken care of, and I should not worry. When I asked if I could see his apartment, he welcomed me in. The place was a pig sty; there was peeling paint and falling plaster, there were obvious areas of roof leaks with buckets to catch the water. A couple of young punks were hanging out. This was apparently a place for them to hang out and do their drugs, drink, and take advantage of this man who was incapable of thinking logically.

I won the bid at the auction for a dollar more. I went back to let the ex-owner know. He was drunk again, or still, and in complete denial about the circumstances. I informed the first floor tenant, who was glad someone responsible was taking over the building to take care of repairs and get rid of the undesireables. She also had the name and number of the ex-owner's daughter. I was able to reach her. She admitted her dad had problems and was hard to talk to. However, she would see what she could do. The day before the eviction he was still in denial and drunk. The daughter said she would come by and pick him up after the eviction. I was relieved about that. I remodeled the building with about $20,000 and sold it for $59,000.

An interesting experience I had with this building was that one of the workers came back to the building after work one day because he had left his lunch box on the second floor, so he says. Since the first floor tenant was not home to let him in the building, he decided to climb up the side of the building to the second floor balcony. When he reached his arm over the side or edge of the balcony, the top stone gave way with his weight on it. He fell to the sidewalk below, hitting his head. When I visited him the next day in the hospital, the surgeons had drilled a hole in his head to relieve pressure on his brain. He still had blurred vision.

He initiated a lawsuit shortly thereafter. They were seeking $100,000 and claiming he was just walking by when a stone fell and hit him on the head. Fortunately, I did have insurance, and a witness across the street saw him going up the side of the building.

If I would not have had insurance, it would have been a nightmare for me. As it was, the insurance company took care of everything. Of course, it also protected my 50% financial partner.

Case in Point # 22, Midlothian

I got a phone call from a lady who had gotten my letter. She was desperate. Her home was scheduled for the auction in two days. You are familiar with the word procrastination. This was not the first last-minute phone call I have gotten.

The value of her home was about $160,000; the mortgage balance was about $90,000. When I say she was desperate, she really was! Her husband was a Police Officer who was not even aware of the problem. She took care of paying the bills, but she had developed a very bad habit; gambling! She kept thinking she would hit it big, until now she was two days away from losing her home and possibly her marriage.

I called a private lender I work with and scheduled an appointment for a couple hours later. I showed up early to make sure she had followed my instructions of having her husband there and informing him about their circumstances. She had, and he was in a stunned state of shock. He did not say anything for about fifteen minutes. I finally asked how he felt about everything. He said he did not really know how to feel. He was stunned and that he did not see how he had a choice. My financial investor showed up, and I left after introducing them. That was how he liked it. He worked out his own sale / lease back with option terms. He paid me a $500 referral.

Case in Point # 23, Markham

This house was another response to one of my mailed letters. The young man was living with his Dad in the home, a three-bedroom brick bungalow with a full basement and a two-car garage. Dad was divorced from Mom. There were two adult sisters and two adult brothers. Dad died. The young man really did not have

The Reality of Real Estate Investing

much besides the house, and Mom's name was still on the title. The mortgage balance was around $10,000, while the value of the house was about $60,000. The son had not made the mortgage payments because he felt the brothers and sisters should help out with the financial responsibility. The home needed about $10,000 in repairs. Of course, the siblings felt, "He lives there; he should take care of it." After much effort in talking and negotiating with each of the siblings and Mom, I finally reached an agreement with everybody.

The young man would have to move out. Then Mom would get $5,000, (Only because she was very stubborn and adamant about it) and I could not tell the siblings what she was getting. Each of them would get $500. We remodeled and sold it for $59,000.

Case in Point # 24, Sauk Village

I was following up on one of my leads. It was probably just a commission earning opportunity. I found a vacant ranch home with a full basement and a two-car garage. I called the attorney representing the bank, just to check if he had a response from the owner and if he knew where he was. He did and agreed to pass my name and number on to him. The owner called me, and I listed the home for $54,900 with a $45,000 simple assumption FHA mortgage. (That means a buyer does not have to qualify to assume the mortgage) It sold right away for $52,000.

At 7% commission, it was not a bad deal at all for an easy sale.

Case in Point # 25, Crete

I pulled up in front of an address that was a foreclosure lead in the first stage. There were people going in and out. It soon became obvious that there was a sale taking place, everything in the house was for sale. He was selling everything and leaving that day to move to Florida. I explained why I was there, and he told me I was not the first, that someone else had just left and they were going to be back in a while with an offer. He allowed me to go ahead and look around, and then I offered him a $1,000 lock, stock, and barrel to sign over a quick claim deed. I put our agreement in writing, gave him $50 to toward the $1,000. His ex-wife was still on the title, per my request he called her and she agreed to meet us at a currency exchange in one hour. I prepared a quick claim deed got the balance of $950 in cash and met them both. He told me the other guy came back wanting to buy the place and he got upset when he was told the home was already sold. The deed was signed and notarized and they each got five hundred dollars. I now had a house with some furniture and miscellaneous items. It was valued at about

Allen Watkins

$60,000 and had a simple assumption mortgage on it which meant that it could be brought current and taken over by anybody without qualifying. The back payments were about $5,000, the principle amount of the mortgage was about $48,000. I ordered the simple assumption package from the lender and ran an ad. I got a buyer right away who gave me $10,000 down and I simply let them step into my shoes for the simple assumption. It never went into my name, I had a deed, but never got around to recording it. The buyers attorney took care of it for me. After it was all said and done I ended up with about $4,000 profit. Not bad for a quick easy deal because I was ready to act quickly.

Glossary Of Real Estate Terms

Adjustable - Rate Mortgage (ARM): A mortgage for which the interest rate and the payments change during the life of the loan.

Amortization: A loan that is completely paid off, interest and principal, by a series of regular payments that are equal or nearly equal.

Appreciation: An increase in the worth or value of a property due to economic or related causes, which may prove to be either temporary or permanent; opposite of depreciation

Capital Gains Tax: The taxable profit derived from the sale of a capital asset. The capital gain is the difference between the sale price and the basis of the property, after making appropriate adjustments for closing costs, fixing up expenses, capital improvements, allowable depreciation, etc.

Closing statement: A detailed cash accounting of a real estate transaction showing all cash received, all charges and credits made and all credits made and all cash paid out in the transaction.

Cloud on title: Any document, claim, un-released lien or encumbrance that may impair the title to real property or make the title doubtful; usually revealed by a title search and removed by either a quitclaim deed or suit to quiet title.

Contingency: A provision in a contract that requires a certain act to be done or a certain event to occur before the contract becomes binding.

Conventional Loan: A loan that is not insured or guaranteed by a government source.

Deficiency judgement: A personal judgement levied against the borrower when a foreclosure sale does not produce sufficient funds to pay the mortgage debt in full.

Dower: The legal right or interest, recognized in some states, that a wife acquires in the property her husband held or acquired during their marriage. During the husband's lifetime the right is only a possibility of an interest; upon his death it can become an interest in land.

Dual agency: Representing both parties to a transaction. This is unethical unless both parties agree to it, and it is illegal in many states.

Earnest Money: The deposit by a potential buyer to show he or she is serious about the property. If the sale is finalized, the money is applied to the down payment.

Easement: A right to use land of another for a specific purpose, such as for a right-of-way or utilities.

Eminent domain: The right of a government or municipal quasi-public body to acquire property for public use through a court action called condemnation,

Allen Watkins

in which the court decides that the use is a public use and determines the compensation to be paid to the owner.

Encroachment: A building or some portion of it; a wall or fence for instance that extends beyond the land of the owner and illegally intrudes on some land of an adjoining owner or a street or alley.

Encumbrance: Anything; such as a mortgage, tax, or judgement lien, an easement, a restriction on the use of the land or an outstanding dower right; that may diminish the value of the property.

Equity: The interest or value which an owner has in real estate over and above the liens against it.

Federal Home Loan Mortgage Corporation (FHLMC or Freddie Mac): A quasi-governmental secondary market agency that purchases whole mortgage loans. Freddie Mac sells interest in pools of mortgage loans to obtain funds for mortgage loan purchases.

Federal Housing Administration (FHA): A government agency within the Department of Housing and Urban Development that administrators many programs involving housing loans made from private funds, including mortgage insurance for lenders and rent or interest assistance for low-income tenants and mortgagors.

Federal National Mortgage Association (Fannie Mae): A privately owned and managed corporation that purchases mortgage loans originated by other lenders. Fannie Mae issues stocks and securities to obtain funds for its purchases.

Fixed Rate Mortgage: A loan that fixes the interest rate at a prescribed rate for the duration of the loan.

Escrow: The deposit of instruments and funds with instructions to a third neutral party bonded by law to carry out the provisions of an agreement or contract.

Evict: The physical removal of a person from a property.

Exchange: The trading of an equity in a piece of property for the equity in another.

Exclusive Right To Sell: A listing in which the owner may sell his property but with the payment of a commission.

Federal Housing Administration (F.H.A.): the federal government agency which administers F.H.A. insured loans.

Federal Tax Lien: An obligation to the United States government as a result of non-payment of taxes.

F.N.M.A.: Abbreviation for the Federal National Mortgage Association. It is an agency which buys big blocks of loans from banks, thus enabling the banks to loan more money. The F.N.M.A. gets its money by selling securities in the market to investors. The securities are guaranteed by the loans behind them.

Forced Sale: An involuntary sale of real property. The owner is forced, usually by law to sell a property for whatever it will bring.

Grantee: The buyer.
Grantor: The seller.
Homestead: A home upon which the owner or owners have recorded a declaration of homestead, which protects the home against judgments up to specified amounts.
Impound account: A compulsory bank account demanded of a borrower by the lender to ensure the payment of taxes and insurance of the property on which the loan was made.
Joint Tenancy: Joint ownership by two or more persons with right of survivorship; all joint tenants own equal interest and have equal rights in the property.
Junior Lien: A lien that does not have first priority, that makes property security for the payment of a debt or discharge of an obligation. Example: judgements, taxes, mortgages, deed of trust, etc. Any lien below the first lien.
Lis Pendens: Suit pending, usually recorded so as to give constructive notice of pending litigation.
Mechanic's Lien: A lien placed on property by laborers and material suppliers who have contributed to a work of improvement.
Mortgage Insurance Premium (MIP): The consideration paid by a mortgagor for mortgage insurance to FHA. It protects the lender from possible loss in the event of a default on a loan.
Note: A unilateral agreement containing a promise of the signer to give a named person or bearer a definite sum of money at a specified date or on demand. The note usually provides for interest, and it is often secured by a trust deed or a mortgage.
Notice of default: A notice filed to show that the borrower under a mortgage or deed of trust is in default (behind on the payments).
Option: A right given a person to buy or lease property within a stated period and given under certain specified terms. The person has the right to buy or sell, but is not required to do so.
Payment Cap: Limits the amount that a monthly payment on an ARM loan can increase at the time of adjustment.
Points: A charge made by a lender. One point equals one percent of the loan. Points are often used to buy down the interest.
Preliminary Title Report: A report from a title company of present condition of title made prior to the issuance of a title policy.
Principal: A person who is acting for himself in a transaction. Also, the full amount of a loan, note, or a debt, exclusive of interest.
Private Mortgage Insurance (PMI): The insurance coverage offered by a private company that protects a lender against loss on a defaulted mortgage loan. Its use is usually limited to loans with high loan-to-value ratios. The borrower pays the premiums.

Rate Cap: Interest rate cap on an ARM loan; it restricts the upward movement of the loan's interest rate at the time of adjustment.

Right of Survivorship: Right to acquire the interest of a deceased joint owner; distinguishing feature of a joint tenancy.

Subordination Clause: A clause in a trust deed or mortgage by which the lender relinquishes his priority to a subsequent trust deed, mortgage, or other lien. It benefits the borrower.

Tenancy in Common: Ownership by two or more persons who hold undivided interest, without right of survivorship; interests need not be equal.

Title: Evidence that an owner of land is in lawful possession; an instrument evidencing such ownership.

Title Insurance: Insurance written by a title company to protect property owners against loss if title is imperfect.

Trustee: One who holds property in trust for another to secure the performance of an obligation.

Trustor: One who deeds his property to a trustee to be held as security until he has performed his obligation to a lender under terms of a deed of trust.

Veterans Administration (VA): A government agency that helps veterans of the armed forces obtain housing.

Epilogue

Failure and Success in one Afternoon
(A true life experience by Allen Watkins)

While serving in the U.S. Navy aboard an aircraft carrier, we had pulled into Quantanomo Bay Cuba after being at sea for three weeks. Some friends and I were out on liberty, which is rare free time in the Navy. My friends persuaded me to go swimming with them down by the cliffs. I should have been enjoying myself, but I felt something was lacking, I wanted something more!

I was the last one in the water, not being excited about the idea in the first place. The ocean floor in this area was really rocky and rough which was uncomfortable to my feet. I decided to get out and just enjoy some sun, sitting among the rocks.

While indulging in some excellent sun rays, I noticed how high, rough, and ragged the cliff walls were. I had feeling of how terrible it would be if someone were to fall from the top, a distance of about fifty feet. For some strange reason I had mixed emotions about the cliffs. I thought to myself, "If a person were to go about it in the right manner and very carefully, he could probably climb the cliffs using the ragged edges as steps and hand holds." A cold chill went up and down my spine and I experienced a feeling of suspense, excitement, danger, and fear! Looking at the different angles, I could visualize myself climbing to the top. I decided to try! While deciding on the best place to begin, an extreme, painful fear entered my head. "What if I were to fall?" That little part of the brain that renders cowardness came forth making me think of the pitiful shape my limp and broken body would be in if I were to fall. I could break my back or my neck. I could die or be crippled for life. I was scared! The challenge of the climb then thrilled me enough to overcome the negative thoughts. I wanted a feeling of successfully defeating something very real and extremely dangerous.

I wanted to prove to myself that I could do it, even though it was risky. It was a feeling of power in over coming my fear.

I walked to the bottom of the cliff, took a deep breath and carefully began my assent. Little by little, slowly and very carefully I progressed upward. I paused to rest about half way up. Looking down, I noticed the people in the immediate area had gathered to watch. Some in amazement, I heard someone say, "He must be crazy or drunk." One guy shouted, "Hey stupid, what are you trying to prove?" I ignored all the comments, and tried to blot the people from my mind.

Many thoughts ran through my mind, especially visualizing myself falling tumbling over and over, crashing into the rocks below. No! I can not think this way, or I will fall. I must think positive. I can make it! I carefully began again.

I was getting closer to the top now. The only parts of my body touching the cliff were my hands and feet which were aching bad now. It would be a bad time to get a cramp. I need to stop thinking this way. I moved cautiously and slowly within a few feet of the top. I began grasping for a hand hold to go that last few feet. I tried every angle possible, but I could not reach anything that would support my weight.

I had a sharp feeling of being stranded. I was in danger. I felt as though I had failed myself. I could not make it and to keep trying would lead me into my last deathly step. I had a feeling of defeat and felt ashamed for even trying. I pulled myself together for the climb back down.

I was trembling all over, especially my knees which felt very weak. I gradually concentrated these weaknesses away as I continued on. When I reached the bottom I sat down and rested in dismay. I did not look around, even though I heard some laughter in the distance. I had never felt the feelings of failure and defeat before as I did at this time, and thinking of the future and how I would feel about this attempt to climb this cliff. Attempt. So far that was all it was however, I could try again. An old cliché came to mind; "If at first you don't succeed, try, try again!" This gave me some confidence.

I examined the cliffs again, visualized a path and began my assent for the second time. As I proceeded upward a rock suddenly gave way under my left hand and went tumbling down. From then on I tested each and every rock by using my strength to pull on it before actually putting my weight on the rocks. A few more rocks gave way as I worked my way to the top. When I was just a couple of feet from the top I was again faced with the dilemma of no hand hold. I was able to move to the right and after a few feet I found a rock that would be a large stretch to reach. It would be risky! However, I had a feeling I could make it and stretched my hand out and firmly grabbed the rock. Then I slowly pulled my way up and over the edge and onto the top of the cliff.

I was exhausted however, I felt a feeling of peace within myself, a feeling of accomplishment. I had succeeded! I stood looking all around, over the massive ocean at the horizon, feeling "Victory!"

It wasn't a great feat to anyone else, however, it was to me. And on that day, that is what counted most.

I hope this book has been an inspiration and a wealth of information for you.

I wish you the best in your endeavors.
We are put here on earth not to see through one another,
we are put here to help see one another through!

The Reality of Real Estate Investing

I would appreciate your comments on what you thought of the book and of your experiences. Please e-mail me; **Allen@HomeBargains.com**

Now that you have read the book, an additional learning experience, and a significant boost to getting you started, is the simulated investment experience described below.

Allen Watkins

The Virtual Reality of Real Estate Investing

A Real Estate Investment
Simulation Experience!

Have fun learning while you play!
Increase your Negotiating Skills Tremendously!
Real life scenarios & facts!

Buy Foreclosures and Bank Owned properties (REO's). Learn how to analyze the numbers, acquire the money, negotiate, bid at auctions, market for fun & profit without the real life risk, Virtually!
Then you can do it for real!

    This game is a superior teaching tool because it requires the players to start with no money and become fully involved in the learning process, while having fun. Playing the game involves a person mentally, emotionally and physically.
    This game is a must for anyone who has, or ever will desire to invest in real estate. Based on real life concepts, a want to be investor becomes one, with out the real life risks. You gain a real life experience for analyzing, negotiating, bidding at auction, working with a financial partner purchasing homes and apartment buildings, working with contractors, being a landlord, and being an entrepreneur by building your own real estate empire.

To order call 219-762-3437 or go to our web site
www.HomeBargains.com

Allen Watkins

About the Author

Allen Watkins
Real Estate Broker / Investor

A rags to financial independence story himself, Allen began his Real Estate career in Chicago in the early 1980's. After quickly losing interest in the typical new Realtor activities, Allen went to work with a Real Estate Broker named Gary Furstenfeld, who became his mentor. He sums up his experience with Gary by quoting an old cliché; "If you feed a man a fish, you feed him for a day. If you teach a man how to fish, you feed him for life!"

With guidance, direction, and Allen's own persistent aggressiveness, he earnestly carved his way into the vast opportunities of dealing with foreclosures and bank-owned properties. His activities ranged from counseling people in foreclosure, (helping them save their equity) to using other people's money (private and cash advances on credit cards), to purchasing property at auctions and from banks.

Having performed tens of millions of dollars in Real Estate transactions and owning over a million dollars worth of rental homes and apartment buildings, from a vacant lot to a 76 unit . Allen expanded his abilities and services in 1991 by starting a real estate brokerage business and developing his niche market in the Realtor Industry, by focusing on marketing properties in foreclosure and bank owned properties. He has published the leading source for bargain properties; **"The Bank Foreclosure / Motivated Seller Report."**

He is the author of the books; "The Reality of Real Estate Investing,"Home Marketing Strategies and The R.E.O. Business Marketing System, and the creator of the real estate investment simulation, a fun and educational board game; "The Virtual Reality of Real Estate Investing."

He has also developed a system for helping retail sellers save thousands of dollars on real estate commissions, while still getting all the benefits of the Realtors' most powerful marketing tool. THE MULTIPLE LISTING SERVICE (M.L.S.) COMPUTER SYSTEM.

His mission is one of service:

- Helping sellers save money & sell quickly.
- Helping investors & bargain home buyers make profitable purchases.
- Working with people in foreclosure to help them sell or refinance to stop the foreclosure.
- Buying properties to fix up and re-sell or rent, for profit.

Allen is co-owner of a real estate company headquartered in downtown Homewood, a south suburb of Chicago, Illinois, called Blue Diamond Realty, Inc. His partner and Co-Broker of that office is Bruce Sonnenberg. Allen is a licensed Real Estate Broker in Illinois and Indiana. His services currently cover the 5 county area around Chicago, Lake, and Porter counties of Northwest Indiana.

He has created a web site which he says is only a fraction of what he has plans for it to become, as time allows for further development. The web address is www.HomeBargains.com.

Allen is the co-founder with his wife and good friend Bonnie Hetland of a non-profit organization; The Housing Resource Center, Inc. Establish in 1999 to focus on providing housing to the disabled and to serve as a referral network for other needed services.

Allen is a family man and enjoys his beautiful wife Debra and 3 sons, Chris, 19; Dexter, 12; Dustin, 10. He is also very active in his church where he serves as the Elders Quorum President and as a Home Teacher. He loves participating in sports such as racquetball, basketball, paintball, little league baseball, and Special Olympics, with his boys, and even plays in a men's Over the Hill baseball league.

Life has it's challenges,

but we settle first,

whether to live to our best

or our worst.

Printed in the United States
3004